MUSTARD

ALSO BY KAT SANDLER

Bang Bang
Punch Up

MUSTARD

KAT SANDLER

PLAYWRIGHTS CANADA PRESS
TORONTO

For professional or amateur production rights, please contact:
Emma Laird at the GGA
250 The Esplanade, Suite 304
Toronto, ON M5A 1J2
416.928.0299, http://ggagency.ca/apply-for-performance-rights/

LIBRARY AND ARCHIVES CANADA CATALOGUING IN PUBLICATION
Sandler, Kat, author
        Mustard / Kat Sandler.

A play.
Issued in print and electronic formats.
ISBN 978-1-77091-921-1 (softcover).--ISBN 978-1-77091-922-8 (PDF).
--ISBN 978-1-77091-923-5 (EPUB).--ISBN 978-1-77091-924-2 (Kindle)

        I. Title.

PS8637.A5455M87 2018   C812'.6   C2018-905301-1
                                               C2018-905302-X

Playwrights Canada Press acknowledges that we operate on land which, for thousands of years, has been the traditional territories of the Mississaugas of the New Credit, Huron-Wendat, Anishinaabe, Métis and Haudenosaunee peoples. Today, this meeting place is home to many Indigenous peoples from across Turtle Island and we are grateful to have the opportunity to work and play here.

We acknowledge the financial support of the Canada Council for the Arts—which last year invested $153 million to bring the arts to Canadians throughout the country—the Ontario Arts Council (OAC), the Ontario Media Development Corporation and the Government of Canada for our publishing activities.

 Canada Council
for the Arts
Conseil des arts
du Canada

 ONTARIO ARTS COUNCIL
CONSEIL DES ARTS DE L'ONTARIO
an Ontario government agency
un organisme du gouvernement de l'Ontario

 Canadä

 Ontario
Ontario Media Development
Corporation

For Mom and Dad for helping
me believe in magic.

For Tom for always helping me
get there.

And for Bozo and Unicorn:
wherever you are, I sincerely hope
you get a kick out of this.

AUTHOR'S NOTE

I had two imaginary friends growing up. One was, simply, Unicorn. Our relationship had two distinguishing features: we loved swinging on swings and I called on Unicorn when I needed to feel brave. Sometimes I still do.

The other was Bozo. Bozo was an elf from the North Pole. He was a fantastic and hilarious character created by my dad by pushing his tongue against his lower lip, thus giving himself a silly voice. He would chat with me like that for a long time, on any number of ridiculous subjects. I don't know why he was Christmas-based (my dad is Jewish . . .) but, suffice it to say, I got a big kick out of hanging with Bozo, because he could *really* talk to me.

When I was around six, my father took me on a canoeing trip, during which I bashed my knee on a rock. There was a ton of blood and I cried and cried, but when Dad rushed over to help, I batted him away. I didn't want him; I wanted Bozo. Inexplicably, Bozo disappeared after that. He was gone for years, so long I almost forgot about him. He eventually made a few appearances in my teens, at dinner parties or as a joke, but it wasn't the same. I wasn't all that interested in the North Pole and a silly voice anymore.

I always wondered where Bozo went for those in-between years. And then I started wondering about what happens to these childhood pals, these creations of our boundless young imaginations, these morale boosters and co-conspirators, when they go away because we think we don't need them anymore, or someone says it's time to grow up. Where *do* they go? What if it isn't a nice place? How far would they go to stay here with us? Would their staying mean that we were crazy? Would that be the *worst* thing? No matter what our age, couldn't we all use someone whose sole purpose is to love us?

The result of this wondering (and a lot of peoples' support and hard work) is *Mustard*.

Mustard imagines a world where everyone on earth is born with a Boon who appears as whatever that child wants to see most—duck, human, robot, etc.—and loves them unconditionally. A Boon lives with their Person until they are no longer needed (usually until their Person grows up), then retires to the Boonswallows, a terrible place where they live out a dark eternity.

Mustard is a comic-tragic play. It is silly at times, but it's also about a lot of very serious and scary things, including divorce, alcoholism, suicide, mental health, teen pregnancy and *growing up*, which can be violent, tragic, funny and magical all at once. That's how this play should feel. For all the poo and fart jokes, *Mustard* is, at its core, a play about love; we're watching real people deal with real problems with real stakes, trying to find ways to love and be loved, and some of those people just happen to be magical. So ultimately a production of this play should try to find a balance somewhere between quick-moving farcical romp, dark fairy tale and modern family drama. Easy peasy, right? Nope, not at all, but here's some potentially useful info!

Sadie and Thai are trying to find a way to adjust to their new reality. Sadie is a desperately sad woman tackling life as a single mom, whose lovelorn depression has become so crippling she's considering suicide. Thai is dealing with all the stress of teenagedom, a newfound inexplicable violent streak and a massive secret she's hidden from everyone around her, and trying to navigate what all that means for her relationship with her older boyfriend. Their scenes should never feel like an after-school special, but should be a snapshot of two women at different stages struggling with the knowledge that life as they knew it is changing forever, and who eventually find strength in their relationship with each other.

Bug and Leslie are former Boons, sent to retrieve Mustard both for outstaying his welcome and appearing to a non-Person. Although they can't physically remove him from our world, they can and do use violence to try to scare him off. They once had Persons themselves, so they do understand what they are asking of Mustard, but as he proves to be a hard nut to crack, they become more frustrated and menacing with each scene they appear in until they are forced to use the most difficult and vicious weapon of all: *reason*.

Bug and Leslie absolutely reference buddy thugs from the movies, but they're not just a comic-relief duo—they are *rule enforcers* and should be truly terrifying at times. They can be nightmarish but shouldn't be cartoonish; they should feel a little bit otherworldly, but not like they're in a completely different play. They take their job *very* seriously, and should exhibit a deep and beautiful camaraderie that suggests many years of working together doing a difficult and thankless task that they find a way to enjoy because . . . what else can they do?

For the record, in our original production, Leslie was the Brit, but either can be British, or neither can, but not both; Bug can sound like he's from Brooklyn, have any accent that works with his text or just be a bit lazy with his words. Either could also be a woman.

Mustard himself is ridiculous, but never ludicrous. He is naive and has a childish energy, but he's not a child (this is not TYA), or a character in a zany sitcom; he is, as Thai imagines him, a grown man with immature, sometimes crass tendencies that mirrored her own as she grew up, and he is her best friend. As far as Mustard knows, he is as real and wise as any of us; he just lives under the bed and doesn't know all the ins and outs of our language or culture, but he's *trying* to learn, while finding the fun in our world that the rest of us grown-ups might miss. He literally lives for Thai, and his unconditional love for her, coupled with his honest desire to help Sadie, should make him real for us too.

Please have so MUCH FUN creating and playing in this world.

And use real Pop Rocks, if you can. They really do sound magical.

NOTES ON PUNCTUATION / PRONUNCIATION / CONVERSATIONS AROUND MUSTARD

A forward slash (/) marks the point in a character's line where the next character begins speaking.

An asterisk (*) at the end of a line is the cue for a character to speak who has an asterisk at the beginning of their line, even though on the page a line or more of dialogue may separate the first character's lines from the response of the second.

When a line appears in SMALL CAPS, it doesn't necessarily mean that it should be yelled, but just given a certain intensity.

Words like *oldmanpoobumbuttmuffin* are meant to be pronounced quickly and fluidly, as close to one word as possible. Words like *klutzbody* are meant to be pronounced like the word "somebody"—so, almost like klutz-*buddy*. Words like *somewhom* should sound more like "someoom" than "someWHOOOM." These guys can *almost* do English, they're just a bit off.

In scenes where people who can't see Mustard speak around him (e.g., Sadie's attempted suicide or Thai and Jay's discussion about the baby) they should never appear to be waiting for him to finish his line, as they cannot hear him.

NOTE ON PACE

Pick it up. Give it all the velocity of adolescence.

Mustard was first produced by Tarragon Theatre, Toronto, in the Extraspace from February 10 to March 13, 2016, with the following cast and creative team:

Mustard: Anand Rajaram
Sadie: Sarah Dodd
Thai: Rebecca Liddiard
Bug: Tony Nappo
Leslie: Julian Richings
Jay: Paolo Santalucia

Director: Ashlie Corcoran
Stage Manager: Nicola Benidickson
Lighting Designers: Graeme S. Thomson and Nick Andison
Set and Costume Designer: Michael Gianfrancesco
Sound Designer: Christopher Stanton

The play was remounted by Tarragon Theatre in January 2018, and was later mounted by the Arts Club Theatre, Vancouver, and the Belfry Theatre, Victoria, in fall 2018.

CHARACTERS

Mustard
Sadie, in her forties or fifties
Thai, sixteen
Bug
Leslie
Jay, twenty

SETTING

A cross-section of a house. A living room / hall, couch, ottoman, chair, coffee table and hutch that acts like a kind of bar. A hall leads off stage to the kitchen. Stairs lead up to a second-floor hall connecting Thai and Sadie's rooms, and a bathroom. The layout should be such that when actors have offstage dialogue, we can still hear them without it seeming too unnatural. We can see into Thai's room—window, bed, bedside table, chair, clothes strewn everywhere and drawings and pictures pasted on the walls in an attempt to cover the old childlike wallpaper. The house should feel very lived in.

Lights up on MUSTARD. *He is very excited but trying to play it cool. He is meeting a baby for the first time, but not necessarily holding it. He may be speaking towards us as if he is looking down into a crib. He wears a superfun hat (maybe it's jingly) and is dressed like a badly drawn cartoon or a child's imaginative version of a funny thing.*

MUSTARD: *(full of wonder)* Woah. *(beat)* You're so little. Oh, wow. I guess I thought your face would look better. I'm sorry, but it just looks like poop. Isn't that the best word—POOP? Oh, this one too. *(whispered) Fuck.* FUCK. Hey, thank you, by the way, for the hat—I really *fucking* love it. *(official)* Okay, little baby, should we get started? *(beat, then it just tumbles out)* I love you. *(embarrassed)* Oh, geez, I was trying to play it cool, but it JUST HIT ME. This is so crazy, like I don't even know you, and I already totally love you forever. For. Ever. Is that one word or two—I don't even know! Hey, do you love me too? Say something, anything. *(beat)* Are you asleep? Have you been asleep this whole time? *(beat, whispered)* Did I already say I love you?

Lights fade. Sixteen years pass in an instant. Lights snap up. We're in a living room. THAI *stands wearing a private school uniform, holding a bloody Kleenex to her nose.* SADIE *is wearing a man's oversized sweater, clutching a glass of wine as she reads a note. It's the middle of the day. Maybe she's a bit drunk.*

SADIE: You *bit* her.

THAI: I bit her.

SADIE: Where?

THAI: The face.

SADIE: The *face. (looking at the letter, resigned)* That's what it says. / The *face.*

THAI: Well . . . the *cheek.* It's not like I bit her face off—I barely even broke the skin—it was / just an intimidation tactic.

SADIE: Okay. *Okay.* OKAY. I'm trying to be understanding. Last week you punched a boy in the ear, / this week you bit a girl in the face.

THAI: Okay, so am I grounded? Am I grounded. Am I *grounded?*

SADIE: Are you troubled?

THAI: What?

SADIE: Are you a troubled teen?*

THAI: What?

SADIE: *Are you doing drugs?

THAI: No! Are *you?* You know, / I see you—

SADIE: Was it something she said?

THAI: No, I wasn't even talking to her, I was talking to . . . / never mind.

SADIE: Who. *Who*. WHO.

THAI: . . . never *MIND*.

Beat. She knows exactly who. They've had this fight before.

SADIE: Oh god, Thai. Honestly, how can this still be going on? I thought you were *better*—you said he was gone, you said he went away!

THAI: Well, I didn't want you to think I was crazy!

SADIE: But you are! You are crazy! You're sixteen years old and you're still "seeing" . . . someone!

THAI: I'm not "seeing him," we're just *hanging out*! I'm going to my room.

THAI goes to her room, slams the door.

SADIE: No, I'm sending you to your room, because you know what, you *are* grounded! Go to your room!

THAI: You can't send me somewhere I already am!

SADIE: You're lucky you even have a room!

Up in her room, THAI takes something out of her knapsack.

THAI: What does that even mean! You're so . . . *You* are crazy. You're the crazy one! You are such a crazy fucking . . . *alcoholic*.

SADIE: THAI.

THAI goes down the hall, into the bathroom.

THAI: You're drunk right now!*

SADIE: NO I AM NOT!

THAI: *And* you're a drug addict!

THAI emerges and throws a bottle of pills at her mother's feet.

SADIE: Those are to help me SLEEP!

SADIE puts them in her sweater.

THAI: The *painkillers* from when you broke your arm? I don't think so! Do you have any idea how messed up it is that YOU'RE lying / to ME about drugs?

SADIE: I'm not lying, and you / don't get to—

THAI: And I hear you, you know, having those "conversations" with "Imaginary Dad."

This sinks in for SADIE.

What, what, it's okay for you to get totally wasted in the afternoon and talk to like, the air, but I can't talk to my REAL friend, who *actually* loves me? *(beat)* That's the difference between you and me, Mom. I fight for the people I love, and you just sit back and let them leave you for *(spits the word)* orthodontists.

THAI goes into the bathroom, slams the door. From bathroom:

JUST SIGN THE PAPERS ALREADY, DAD'S FUCKING GONE.

SADIE goes to the bathroom, knocks on the door.

SADIE: Thai! I want to talk about this! You come out here right now! Thai! THAI.

SADIE goes to her own room in a huff. Slams the door. Toilet flushes.
THAI peeks out of the bathroom, something in her hand, goes to her
room and sits on the end of the bed holding a home pregnancy test.
We hear growling or funny noises, a metaphorical drum roll from
under the bed; someone's about to make an entrance . . .

THAI: Stop.

MUSTARD: *(in a funny voice, unseen)* I'm the monster under the bed . . .

THAI: Stop it!

MUSTARD: . . . and I'm going to poop all over your head!

MUSTARD emerges from under the bed with his hat. Ta-da! It's a big
production. THAI shoves the test in a drawer, takes out her sketchbook.

Hey, look what I found! Remember this? I forgot how much I love this fucking hat! What's wrong?

THAI: Nothing.

MUSTARD: Then quit being a bitchfacepoogrump and play with me! What? What is it?

THAI: I don't want you to come to school anymore.

MUSTARD: I didn't even do anything! You were the one that bit that girl's face, and it was *(with glee)* DISGUSTING.

THAI: So you LEFT? I didn't even know you could do that—just . . . leave and go somewhere by yourself. You're supposed to do what I want to do.

MUSTARD: Hey, we're supposed do things *together*. What's up with you?

THAI: The Saddest Sad is just being a huge bitch; she does *not* know how to cope with the divorce.

MUSTARD: Cope?

THAI is sick of explaining stuff like this.

THAI: Cope, *coping*, bottling up your shit and pretending it's not a problem.

MUSTARD: Maybe she just needs help.

THAI: Well, it's not my job to help her: she's a mom, she's just supposed to be *fine*.

MUSTARD: This is all stupidface Bruce's fault—*

THAI: *(to herself)* No, it's not.

MUSTARD: *—stupidface—one word?

THAI: It's not / a word.

MUSTARD: Should be.

THAI: No, it's . . . fuck! It's not like he's dead—he just *left*, and Mom won't sign the divorce papers. Like, grow up, I miss him too.

MUSTARD: Hey, does signing the papers make you stop loving someone?

THAI: No, it just means you give them half your stuff.

MUSTARD: Yeah, but does she / still love—

THAI: ARRG, MUSTARD.

MUSTARD: WHAT?

THAI: Can we just . . . not talk for a bit?

They sit in silence. MUSTARD makes an annoying sound, blows in her ear, something smallish yet completely infuriating. If you have a sibling, you'll know what this is.

ARRRG. MUSTARD.

MUSTARD: What, I'm not talking!

THAI gets a text.

Is that oldmanpoobum Jay?

THAI: Yes, stop calling him that.

MUSTARD: I don't know why you like him, he's like a million years old and he looks like an armpit.

THAI starts changing out of her uniform. Her regular clothes are much more alternative, punk lite.

THAI: I think he's romantic.

MUSTARD: Oh yeah, it's so romantic that he calls you "milady," and puts his jacket over puddles for you—I mean, you can *see* the puddles, you have EYES.

THAI: *(answering text)* I'm going out.

MUSTARD: Right now? I don't want to go out.

THAI: Well, you're not invited.

Indignation from MUSTARD.

What? You didn't want to be at the fight, I don't want you to come out tonight.

MUSTARD: You're being an *asshole*, you know that?

THAI: *You're* being an asshole!

MUSTARD: Come on. Don't go out with that oldmanpoobumbuttmuffin. Those pants are too tight and your hair looks like a fart.

He ruffles her hair, she bats him away.

THAI: Arrg! Mustard! Have fun being alone under the bed!

MUSTARD: I'm gonna tell everybody you're having the sex with a wrinkly old asscabbage!

THAI: *(on her way out)* Yeah, well good luck because nobody else can *see you.*

She starts climbing out the window. SADIE comes to THAI's door.

SADIE: Thai?

MUSTARD: Your mom!

THAI: Fuck her.

She goes.

SADIE: Can I come in?

MUSTARD: Nooo . . . !

SADIE is about to open the door. MUSTARD goes to the door, holds it shut. He panics, grabs THAI's sketchbook and scribbles on a piece of paper.

SADIE: I'm sorry about earlier. I just . . . I just want you to know that I love you, okay? No matter how many faces you bite. No matter how many imaginary friends you have, I am your mother, and I will always love you. Okay? Thai?

Beat.

MUSTARD: *(to door)* Just so you know, she loves you too. Very much.

MUSTARD rips the page out and slides the note under the door. SADIE picks up the note from the ground, reveals it to us. It reads "FUCK YOU" in giant letters. SADIE dejectedly heads down the stairs, pours a glass of wine (probably from a box . . .), grabs the divorce papers, looks at them sadly. She conjures the image of her ex-husband, BRUCE, and speaks to him as if he is there.

SADIE: Do you remember when we met? Outside that party, a million and one years ago. You asked me how much a polar bear weighs. And I said . . . enough to break the ice.

MUSTARD giggles. SADIE lays the divorce papers out on the coffee table. She pulls the bottle of pills out of her sweater, makes a decision and begins lining them up on the divorce papers. MUSTARD watches her.

And we laughed and laughed at your terrible jokes for an hour. *(taking a pill)* Why is the nose in the middle of the face?

MUSTARD: Why?

SADIE: . . . Because it's the SCENTer.

Another pill. MUSTARD *gets the joke and laughs.*

And you told me you liked to collect flashlights. *Vintage flashlights.* Because you said the only thing worse than being alone is being alone in the dark.

MUSTARD: That's very true.

SADIE: And then you kissed me.

She crumples up the divorce papers in tears.

MUSTARD: Stop. Stop it. No! Hey, I know what you're doing.

SADIE: And this . . . *(another pill)* None of this is for *you*.

MUSTARD: Think about Thai!

SADIE: It's not like I can't live without / you.*

MUSTARD: Thai! *(going to window, whispering)* Thai!

SADIE: *People live without things all the time . . .

MUSTARD: Thai! Come back!

SADIE: Red meat, dairy, gluten . . .

MUSTARD: Thai!

SADIE: *(devastated)* Sex.

    MUSTARD *gives up, comes back to the living room, watches her pick up the remaining pills in a big handful.*

People live without things all the time . . .

MUSTARD: *(psyching himself up)* Okay . . .

SADIE: I just don't want to.

MUSTARD: . . . Here goes nothing:

> *SADIE puts all the pills in her mouth, is about to swallow, when MUSTARD yells directly in her face.*

STOP!

> *Suddenly she is able to hear him. She turns to him, pills in her mouth. Sees him. Beat. The pills fall out of her mouth. She screams, spits out the remaining pills. MUSTARD screams too.*

SADIE: WHO THE FUCK ARE YOU?

MUSTARD: YOU CAN SEE ME?

SADIE: OHMYGOD! Have you been here the whole time?

MUSTARD: Yes. Well. No . . . / but—

SADIE: Watching me?

MUSTARD: Yes / but not—

SADIE: I'm calling the police!

MUSTARD: Well good, I hope they take all your dumb pills away! What are you trying to do, kill yourself?

SADIE: Yes!

MUSTARD: Why?

SADIE: It's a cry for help!

MUSTARD: Well, then you have to do it with people around!

SADIE: My daughter is upstairs!

MUSTARD: Nope.

SADIE: What?

MUSTARD: Well, she climbed out the window, but I don't know where she ended up.

SADIE: But she's grounded!

MUSTARD: That's like saying she's a zucchini.

SADIE: She wrote me that note!

MUSTARD: No, I wrote that. Sorry. I panicked.

SADIE: What were you doing in her room?

MUSTARD: I live there, okay? / Let's just calm down—

SADIE: IN HER ROOM? YOU LIVE IN HER ROOM?

MUSTARD: No, I live under the bed.

Beat.

SADIE: (as if she's dropped into another dimension) Am I dead?

MUSTARD: No! Not yet. You will be . . .

A terrified look or sound from SADIE.

Oh, no, no, no, I mean one day. I'm not going to kill you right now.

SADIE *screams.*

Or ever. EVER, I'm not going to kill you EVER. *Ever.*

SADIE *is staring at him, as if recognizing something familiar.*

What?

SADIE: It's just . . .

MUSTARD: What?

SADIE: You look a little like my ex-husband.

MUSTARD: NO! No way. Bruce? Blechh. Oh, geez, no, not AT ALL. I mean, we both have noses / but I don't—

Maybe SADIE *slaps herself, hard.*

SADIE: *(as if she's figured it out)* No, I'm *drunk.* And . . . high. The pills . . . and the wine . . . Where did you come from?

MUSTARD: Upstairs. Oh, do you mean originally? I don't know, we just wake up here, so this is my *home* / although it depends on your definition of—

SADIE: I'm sorry. I'm sorry, I'm so sorry, can you just stop talking . . . just for a second?

He stops. Beat.

I'm just going to ask this . . . Are you . . . him? You're . . . *him.*

MUSTARD is nodding gleefully.

Are you . . . Mustard?

MUSTARD: Yeah!

SADIE freaks out, maybe puts her head between the couch cushions.

Yes! And you can tell me your name, but I know it already, so that would be SUPER fluous. Sorry, superfluous. One word. But you can, and then we can shake hands, because wouldn't that be *superfun*, so, *(presentational)* here is my hand to shake hello to be people who know each other!

He offers his hand to shake hello.

SADIE: You are my daughter's imaginary friend.

MUSTARD: No, I am her *best* friend.

SADIE: Who happens to look a lot like her father.

MUSTARD: No I *don't*. Our eyebrows are / completely different.

SADIE: You're her imaginary friend.

MUSTARD: No, *Boon*. I'm her Boon. That's what I am.

SADIE: *Boon.*

MUSTARD: One Boon per kid per household. Except the babies that look like angry old men—they grow up to be lawyers, so we don't bother. You can lead a horse to water but he's not gonna bring a bucket. *(knowingly)* That's a saying. You had one.

SADIE: A horse?

MUSTARD: A Boon!

Beat.

SADIE: Duck Duck?

MUSTARD: Yeah, Duck Duck—she's the *best*, really dry sense of humour.

SADIE: You know her?

MUSTARD: Oh, yeah, we're pals—what a *riot*! TWO sparkly duck heads—you were kind of a strange kid, huh?

SADIE: How is she?

MUSTARD: Oh, she, um, went blind, actually. Well, half-blind—blind in one head. She still comes to visit you sometimes, but you don't see her anymore, so she just stares at you with her one good head—we play a quick round of poker, she gets glitter EVERYWHERE, then she heads back. You look like you're gonna pass out.

SADIE: You are not happening. You are . . . a hallucination, a prank. A man off the street—a burglar, maybe.

MUSTARD: Oh yeah, and what, I just happen to know secret things about you and your family? Like you keep your vibrating rabbit toy in the fourth drawer in your bedroom.

SADIE: Lots of people have vibrators.

MUSTARD: Like Thai is totally terrified of dentists? Oh, like Bruce left a year ago but he still hasn't come back for those old flashlights? Ooh, like you kept that sweater of his and you wear it pretty much every day.

SADIE: Okay, okay. Okay. Why aren't you a bunny or a unicorn or dinosaur?

MUSTARD: This is what Thai wants to see so this is what I look like. Sometimes she draws me new clothes, *(a bit embarrassed)* but she hasn't done that in a while . . . Hey—you wanted to see an adorable two-headed duck MADE OF GLITTER. That's a whole lot weirder if you ask me. I think I look . . . I think I look pretty good.

SADIE: You do. I mean, you look good. Fine, you / look fine.

MUSTARD: Anyway, I really don't think you should kill yourself over stupid-face Bruce. It's just a huge waste of this nice world you live in that smells like peaches and fabric softener and library books and you were going to just throw that all away and leave Thai in the dark because someone stopped loving you?

SADIE: I was just . . . scared, / I guess.

MUSTARD: Yeah, well, just stop being a *scary* cat*

SADIE: What?

MUSTARD: *and just start bottling everything up.

SADIE: *What?*

MUSTARD: COPING, okay? You can't kill yourself. Thai's fucked up enough—biting girls' faces, and punching boys' ears, and climbing out the window to go out with that oldmanpoobumasshat boyfriend of hers.

SADIE: Boyfriend?*

MUSTARD: Whoopsies.

SADIE: *Why didn't she tell me?

MUSTARD: It's kind of hard to get a word in edgewise around all your sad. You know, Bruce was not that great. I know Thai idolated / him, but*

SADIE: Idolized.

MUSTARD: *honestly, I was here, and I'm glad he's gone, because he was the fucking worst and you just remember him wrong. You are pretty and smart and nice and you can do better, so just sign those lovestopping papers already. Honestly, I think he loved those flashlights more than he loved you.

SADIE: Okay. That's enough. You can go now.

MUSTARD: . . . Go?

SADIE: Disappear, or whatever you do. This is a drug-induced hallucination, so you just . . . go now. Vanish. Begone!

MUSTARD: Be gone? What does that even mean? Where would I even bego?

SADIE: It means we're done talking. So undo . . . this.

MUSTARD: I don't know how to undo it. Maybe YOU did it.

SADIE: Okay, fine, I am just going to pretend I never saw you. I am not going to talk to you or acknowledge you until you go away.

MUSTARD: Even when I do this?

> *He does something ridiculous and unignorable. Maybe he pretends to be a cat prowling along the top of the couch, then hacks up a giant hairball. Or something. You get the idea.*

Geez, you know what, I'm sorry—I thought I SAVED YOUR SUPER SAD LIFE. I'm going to my room.

SADIE: It's not your room, it's *my room*!

MUSTARD: It's *Thai's* room!

SADIE: In *my* house!

MUSTARD: Come on, I *live* there.

SADIE: Well, you can't live there anymore. I forbid it!

MUSTARD: *Forbid* it? Where am I supposed to go?

SADIE: I don't care! It's not appropriate for Thai to have a grown man sleeping under her bed—

MUSTARD: Where else would/ I sleep?

SADIE: —watching her change or / whatever!

MUSTARD: Oh, gross, I would never want to see any of her lady bits!

SADIE: AND MY LIFE IS NOT *SAD*.

MUSTARD: AND I'M MADE OF BABY LOBSTERS.

SADIE: GET OUT.

MUSTARD: FINE.

MUSTARD starts to say something else, but SADIE slams the front door in his face. She could nap on the couch or go off stage. On another part of the stage, BUG and LESLIE appear. They look like slightly otherworldly villains, drawn from things that children are afraid of, somewhere between burglars, surgeons, dentists and Dickensian thugs. They could be dressed in a mishmash of time with understated period pieces (e.g., greatcoat) or in simple, slick dark modern suits, but they should look scary. Maybe they have some kind of eye protection—goggles or sunglasses—which can be removed. LESLIE *looks like he is in charge, and* BUG *is more of his assistant, carrying a huge ominous-looking bag. They seem to be casing the house.* BUG *takes a range of exceptionally terrifying tools out of the bag, polishes them and replaces them. Though they can interact with things in the house, the pair of them feel not quite real.*

BUG: It's happening again, Leslie.

LESLIE: Here we are, Bug.

BUG: It's a bit like a vacation, i'n't it?

LESLIE: No it's not—it's not like a vacation: it's our job.

BUG: Yeah, but it's nice, you know, gives us something to do.

LESLIE: True. Otherwise we'd be out of practise. It has been a long while since one of them tried this.

BUG: Yeah, and this guy's made himself real comfortable, di'n't he? I mean, she's *(incredulous) sixteen years old.* And now *this*? You know, I almost feel bad for the guy. Maybe we shoulda got here sooner.

LESLIE: You can't be too hard on yourself. We're here now.

BUG: I'm not even sure I remember the order of things. How it goes.

LESLIE: You will, don't worry—an elephant never forgets how to ride a bicycle.

Blank look from BUG.

That's a *saying*, Bug.

BUG: Right.

LESLIE: And don't worry, I'm here—I'll help you.

BUG: Thank you, Leslie.

LESLIE: You're very welcome, Bug.

> BUG *continues taking out ominous-looking tools, examining or cleaning or sharpening them.*

BUG: So, let's see, we start with the . . . fingernails, yeah?

LESLIE: Right. Best to start with the fingernails.

BUG: Run something very sharp under the edges *(holds up a sharp thing)*, give 'em a good tug: they pop right off.

LESLIE: Right off.

BUG: Like a pop can. *(makes sound)* Pzzzzz.

LESLIE: Always better to work from the outside in.

BUG: Cuz if you start with the insides, 's over too quick. Fingernails first.

LESLIE: See? You remembered perfectly. And then?

BUG: Well . . . Then . . . *(with glee and menace, it comes to him)* We hang 'em off the Tree.

LESLIE: Right. Very good.

BUG: Then we do all the little bones in the fingers, all the little fingerbones.

LESLIE: And then?

BUG: We hang *them* off the Tree!

LESLIE: And the skin, Bug, don't forget the skins.

BUG: *(fondly)* How could I forget all those little fingerskins? One word or two?

LESLIE: Fingerskins. / Finger skins.

BUG: Finger skins. / Fingerskins.

LESLIE: Fingerskins. Fingerskins. One, / I think.

BUG: One sounds about right.

LESLIE: What about faceskin?

BUG: *(thinks)* Oh, that's not till near the end. You gotta keep the face intact so's the mouth can open and close and make all the little scream sounds, *(makes little noises)*, then, at the end, we hang *it* off the / tree—

LESLIE: Yes, very good, but one word or two?

BUG: Faceskin. Face skin. / Faceskin.

LESLIE: Faceskin. / Face skin. Face skin.

BUG: One. One? / One.

LESLIE: One. Yes, one, I think.

BUG: *(hopefully)* Think it'll get to the faceskin?

LESLIE: Alas, it hardly ever gets to the faceskin.

They go into the house through the window, into THAI's room, surround the bed as if they expect to find something underneath it.

BUG: You know, Leslie, 's funny. All these words for the things that makes something up, when underneath it's all just one thing, i'n't it?

LESLIE: What's that, Bug?

BUG: Red. I'n't it?

LESLIE: Red indeed. Shall we get to work? We are on a schedule.

BUG: 'S about time, Leslie.

LESLIE: It's about time.

They pull the covers up to look under the bed and seem surprised to find nothing. They move through the house, go out the front door. Time passes. Morning. We see THAI climb back in the window. She checks the pregnancy test in the drawer, reacts to what she sees. She lies on the bed, starts to cry silently, pulls the covers over her. MUSTARD comes in the front door, terrified, with bloody fingers (or badly bandaged bloody fingers). He sees SADIE sleeping on the couch, goes over and stands over her. Maybe smooths his hair a bit. Then:

MUSTARD: CAN YOU STILL HEAR ME!

SADIE: *(hungover)* What / yes—

MUSTARD: CAN YOU STILL SEE ME?

SADIE: YES. Yes. Oh god, I thought you were a dream. What happened to your hands?

MUSTARD: Nothing.

SADIE: Is that blood?

MUSTARD: Oh, uh, it's not real, it's for a game.

SADIE: What / game?

MUSTARD: *(gesturing to scattered pills)* Look, I don't think Thai should see all this.

SADIE begins picking up the pills.

SADIE: You're right.

MUSTARD: Or, you know, know that we talked to each other and that you can see me, or whatever. I just think it would be really confusing. For her. Just for now. While we're figuring stuff out between us.

SADIE: There is no—

MUSTARD: Hey, can I borrow these mittens forever?

SADIE: Sure . . .

MUSTARD: So . . . you should probably go out with Thai today, and, like, talk to her about stuff.

SADIE: Like what?

MUSTARD: Her super-secret oldmanpoobumboyfriend. Stuff like that. Be a parent, or whatever. That might be fun.

SADIE: Thanks, but I don't need parenting advice from you.

MUSTARD: Actually, I think that's exactly what you need, because, no offence, but you're not doing a very good job. Like if this was your job, you'd be fired. And my advice is to take her to brunch. It's like the only thing you guys still do together.

SADIE: I don't think she'll want to go with me.

MUSTARD: Just ask her!

SADIE: Oh yeah? *(doubtfully)* THAI? DO YOU WANT TO GO TO BRUNCH?

Beat.

THAI: *(from her room)* I THOUGHT I WAS GROUNDED.

SADIE is surprised. MUSTARD gives her the thumbs up.

SADIE: I'LL MAKE AN EXCEPTION.

THAI: THAT WOULD BE . . . NICE.

MUSTARD: See?

THAI: I'M JUST GOING TO HAVE A SHOWER.

SADIE realizes THAI will have to go through the hall and will see MUSTARD.

SADIE: *(to MUSTARD)* Hide!

MUSTARD: What?

SADIE: *Hide!*

MUSTARD hides. THAI goes through the hallway, shoots an awkward look at SADIE, who's doing a terrible job of pretending everything's normal. Maybe THAI *even sees* MUSTARD *hiding stupidly and assumes he's just playing a dumb game, rolls her eyes and goes into the bathroom.* MUSTARD *only comes out of hiding when the shower comes on.*

MUSTARD: Ummm . . . so, okay, have fun. Have a nice day. *(brightly)* Begone.

He awkwardly knocks a photo in a frame, breaking it.

Arg! Sorry—I'm a such a klutzbody.

SADIE: That's okay, I hate that picture anyway.

MUSTARD: Yeah, his face looks dumb. He's got a big dumb face. And dumb eyes.

SADIE: They are dumb eyes.

She looks into MUSTARD's *eyes, and then looks away.*

Don't you have somewhere to be?

MUSTARD *whispers conspiratorially, as if* BUG *and* LESLIE *might hear.*

MUSTARD: Between you and me, most of us are in the Boonswallows by now.

SADIE: Well, don't let me keep you.

MUSTARD: Oh, no, I do NOT want to go there. *(by way of explanation)* It's very dark. *(beat, then, too brightly)* But you know what? Thai doesn't ever want me to go . . . So. *(beat)* She is a *wonderful* Person, Mrs. Collins—really she is, and I loved her from the moment I saw her dumb, dumb face.

Beat.

SADIE: Me too. *(remembering)* But it's *Fray.* It's Fray again so you should call me Ms. Fray.

MUSTARD: Oh, we just call you the Saddest Sad. / Whoopsies.

SADIE: Okay, okay, no. You can just call me Sadie.

MUSTARD: Sadie. I'm Mustard.

He offers his hand. She takes it, reluctantly, and they shake. There's something odd and magical in meeting a thing you thought you could never see, or a person you thought could never see you. It's a bit of a moment until she breaks it.

SADIE: Oh god, is this normal? Are Persons' . . . parents . . . supposed to see you?

MUSTARD: Oh, *no*, not *at all*. It's super weirdfreaky and against all the rules.

SADIE: The *rules*?

MUSTARD: Oh, yeah, it's bad, very very very bad, but you know, I just can't seem to turn it off! You're *special*.

THAI: ALMOST READY, MOM.

SADIE: Right. *I'm* special.

MUSTARD: No, you are. Remember that time Thai fell into the duck pond at that fancy golf-course birthday party with all the fancy moms and their little girls in too-tight braids. And she was covered in pond gunk and goose poo, and you just got up and jumped in and said it was time for a swim, and all the other little girls jumped in too, before their grumpy bitchface moms could stop them. That was pretty special.

SADIE: You were there?

MUSTARD: Are you kidding me—I pushed her in! That was a great day.

They laugh together.

SADIE: I am crazy.

MUSTARD: Maybe. But crazy is fun.

SADIE: Said no man, ever . . . *(trying to nonchalantly change the subject)* God, she takes forever to get ready. *(yelling upstairs)* THAI?

MUSTARD: Okay, here it goes. / I like you.

SADIE: *(to THAI)* The lineup is going to be crazy no matter / where we go!

MUSTARD: I like you. I like you. / I like you.

SADIE: *(to MUSTARD)* Sorry, what? *(to THAI)* THAI!

MUSTARD: I LIKE YOU. I mean, I have liked you. / I've *been* liking you. For a while now.* Even though you're sad.

THAI: Sorry, sorry I'm COMING!

SADIE: *Umm . . . I like you too. But maybe when Thai comes down we shouldn't / be talking.

MUSTARD: Oh geez, I don't know how / to do this.

SADIE: You should go. Maybe / I'll see you around, I guess.

MUSTARD: Would you maybe wanna go out sometime?

SADIE: What?

MUSTARD: Never mind. Nothing.

SADIE: Did you—

MUSTARD: No . . .

THAI: CAN WE GO TO THE ONE WITH THE CHEDDAR WAFFLES?

MUSTARD: *(mock amazement) Cheddar waffles?!*

SADIE: *(to MUSTARD)* Did you just say, "Do you wanna go out sometime"?

MUSTARD: *No!* *(beat)* No. No, no, no. / No.

SADIE: No?

MUSTARD: Yes. Yes, I did. Would you maybe want to go out . . . with me?

SADIE: *With . . . you?*

MUSTARD: Sorry, maybe you're seeing someone / else—

SADIE: *(laughing hysterically)* I am. I'm seeing you. I mean, seeing in the way / that—

MUSTARD: No, I understand, it's a joke. You're making a joke, / I get it—

SADIE: So I don't think / it's a good idea—

MUSTARD: Yeah, forget I said anything, just forget it.

THAI: MOM?

SADIE: WE CAN GO WHEREVER YOU WANT. *(to MUSTARD)* It's . . . because I haven't really started dating again, and Bruce only left—

MUSTARD: A YEAR ago. Maybe it's time to move on!

SADIE: Pardon me?

MUSTARD: No, I get it, it's okay, because you're Thai's mom, and it would be / super weird.

SADIE: No, it's because I don't know if you're REAL.

MUSTARD: *(angrily)* Yeah, I can see how that would not be ideal for like a DATE / SITUATION!

SADIE: Keep your voice down!

MUSTARD: *(angry whisper)* Why? *She* knows I exist!

SADIE: *(angry whisper)* Like, where would we even go, to dinner in the sky? On a cloud?

MUSTARD: I'm not Peter Pan, / I can't FLY!

SADIE: And maybe, I dunno, maybe you bring me flowers, they turn into . . . stars or / something.

MUSTARD: Oh, now you want star flowers? Make up your mind!

SADIE: Can you do that? Do you have those?

MUSTARD: Well, you'll never know now, will you? You've fucked that up royally. No star flowers for you, ever!

SADIE: I'm sorry. I really, really am, but I cannot go out with something that isn't there—I wish I could!

MUSTARD: Why do people *say* that—you *can*, I'm *here*, you're just NOT GOING TO! I'll be under the bed if you need me.

He heads upstairs.

SADIE: Where would you even take me? Never Never Land?

MUSTARD: Never never mind!

SADIE: I NEVER NEVER WILL!

He goes into THAI's room and slams the door. THAI comes out of the bathroom.

THAI: Who are you talking to?

SADIE: My imaginary husband. Right, we are going for brunch and we are getting waffles and we are having a serious discussion about your boyfriend, okay?

THAI: . . . I don't have a / boyfriend.

SADIE: Yes you do! And starting right now, we are going to talk about REAL things in this house, *(for MUSTARD's benefit)* only REAL THINGS that exist in REAL LIFE, BECAUSE EVERYTHING ELSE IS MADE UP, OKAY?

Indignation from MUSTARD.

THAI: . . . Okay, I have a boyfriend.

SADIE: Okay, I wanna hear all about him!

THAI goes out first. SADIE turns back to the house. MUSTARD opens THAI's door.

(angry whisper) Goodbye!

MUSTARD: *(angry whisper)* BEGONE. Have a nice brunch!

SADIE: I WILL.

> *SADIE goes. BUG and LESLIE appear. MUSTARD senses them in the house. He shuts the door to THAI's room, looks for somewhere to hide. They wander about, touching things, moving them slightly, looking for a hiding place. Maybe BUG uncrumples the divorce papers, lays them flat.*

BUG: I have to say, Leslie—I didn't think we'd be back so quick. Didn't think it would take *two* times.

LESLIE: It is unexpected.

BUG: You know, I get a little . . . agitated when we're running behind schedule.

LESLIE: I know, Bug, but if everything went perfectly the first time, there'd be no room for improvisation.

BUG: Yeah, sure, but why do they even try, Leslie, to stay where they don't belong anymore?

LESLIE: Well, they don't want to go. They want to be *kept*.

BUG: Kept by who?

> *MUSTARD hides under the bed.*

LESLIE: Whom. You see, that's exactly the problem; after a certain point, there is nowhom to keep them.

BUG: Nowhom can't be right. Nowhom? / Nowhom.

LESLIE: Nowhom. Nowhom—like nowhere—I think it is, Bug. At the end of the day, there's nowhere to hide, nowhat to do and nowhom to keep them, and yet they keep trying . . .

BUG picks something up, a childhood toy or stuffy, tosses it up and down nonchalantly.

BUG: How many warnings you think a Boon should get, Leslie?

LESLIE: One, I think, Bug.

BUG: Two, *I* think—I don't like to make a mess when there's no mess to be made.

LESLIE: You don't?

BUG: I don't, no, not all the time, and . . .

LESLIE: And?

They're almost at MUSTARD's hiding spot, telegraphing a coordinated strike silently to one another.

BUG: AND, when there's already been one warning, the second warning can be stronger, cuz you were so gentle the first time. Although—

LESLIE: Although?

BUG: Although, it does make a somewhom feel . . . uneffectual—

LESLIE: *In*effectual, but very good, Bug.

BUG: Thank you, Leslie, because it meant the first warning wasn't good enough—he didn't *listen*.

LESLIE: So the second warning is nowhom's fault but his own.

They strike. MUSTARD *is yanked from his hiding place. They stuff the toy into his mouth to gag him, throw him into a chair, restrain him.*

MUSTARD: Help! Help!

LESLIE: Do you think he needs all his teeth?

MUSTARD *screams into his gag.*

BUG: Nah.

LESLIE: Seems to me, if *we're* so *ineffectual*, we might take with us something else that's *ineffectual*.

BUG: Doesn't seem to me that all the teeth can be *fectual*, does it? Fectual?

MUSTARD *screams into his gag.*

LESLIE: That doesn't sound quite right, Bug. Fectual?

BUG: Yeah, fectual, anyway, he certainly don't need all those ones 'n the back. The ones that don't make a difference when you smile, but not having them affects you somehow. Like taking a toe—you'd never know.

LESLIE: But it would affect your balance.

BUG: Plenty of teeth in the mouth, though. Easy to lose one, to misplace it. Hey, kids do it all the time—that's the tooth fairy's whole job.

LESLIE takes out some kind of terrifying tooth extraction device.

LESLIE: Don't be silly, Bug. The tooth fairy isn't real.

They take a tooth. It's awful.

BUG: Should we take a toe as well?

LESLIE: No. He gets the idea, I think.

BUG: Right. Wouldn't want to affect his balance. Lotta things to take into account.

They leave THAI's room, go back through the house. MUSTARD is in excruciating pain.

LESLIE: It's a very delicate process, Bug.

MUSTARD crawls under the bed.

BUG: Yeah. Delicate.

LESLIE thinks, enjoys setting up the game.

LESLIE: Like . . . a *teacup.*

BUG: Heh. Like . . . *(proud) butterfly wings.*

LESLIE: Like . . . a *pressure cooker.*

BUG: That's not very delicate, Leslie.

LESLIE: Oh, yes it is, Bug. At the end of the day, the meat just *falls off the bone.*

BUG: *(admiration)* Oh, you . . .

> *They exit. Time passes.* JAY *and* THAI *come through the window into* THAI'S *room.* THAI *hands him the pregnancy test.* JAY *stares at it. His life flashes before his eyes.* MUSTARD *is under the bed at the beginning of the scene.* THAI *has a black eye.* JAY *can't see or hear* MUSTARD *and so never waits for him to speak. Because* THAI *can see* MUSTARD, *she has a harder time not talking directly to him.*

JAY: How many lines is—?

THAI: Two. / Two.

JAY: *(relieved)* Oh. Okay. / Okay.

THAI: . . . So?

JAY: *(quietly, relieved)* Who-hoo.

THAI: There are two lines there, Jay.

JAY: No . . .

THAI: Are you blind? There's totally two! Look: one, two.

JAY: Oh. *(looking close)* Oh. Oh, god. Yeah.

THAI: *(to JAY)* What's wrong?

JAY: Sorry, everything's a bit blurry.*

THAI: Jay?

JAY: *I'm just feeling a bit faint.

THAI: Jay?

JAY: I think I might pass out.

THAI: Jay?

JAY exhales loudly, emits a short, low scream.

JAY: No, I'm fine, how are you? Should you be standing?*

THAI: I'm fine.

JAY: *I still don't understand what happened to your eye.

THAI: I . . . slipped in the shower.

JAY: Oh, are you—oh shit, ohmygod— Is the *baby* okay?*

MUSTARD mutters from under the bed with cotton balls in his mouth to staunch the bleeding:

MUSTARD: Baby . . . ?

THAI: *Yeah, probably. It's not even a baby yet.

MUSTARD comes out from under the bed, removes cotton balls, throws them under the bed.

MUSTARD: BABY?

THAI: *(trying a joke)* Anyway, I didn't fall on my uterus.

MUSTARD: *(in awe)* We're having a baby?

JAY: *(suddenly ill)* Oh god.

MUSTARD: *(stupefied, eyeing the pregnancy test)* This thing tells you when you're gonna have a BABY?

JAY: Ohmygod.

MUSTARD: How does it even *know?*

JAY: I don't understand, we always used / protection—

THAI: I don't know either, okay? Sometimes shit happens when it's not supposed to, and now we just have to deal with the shit.

MUSTARD: *(touched, excited)* We're having a baby!?

JAY: I guess . . .

MUSTARD: *(to pregnancy test, as if to a walkie-talkie)* I'D LIKE A LITTLE SISTER PLEASE.

JAY: . . . Thank you for telling me?

THAI: You're . . . welcome? I guess?

MUSTARD: *(overjoyed)* We're having a baby!

JAY: So . . . what do you want *me* to do?

THAI: Do?

JAY: Sorry, I didn't mean / for it—

THAI: . . . Nothing. Nothing / at all.

JAY: I mean do you want to . . . get married or something? I'm still in school / so it—

MUSTARD: WOAH. MARRIED? / NO. No, no, no.

THAI: Are you fucking / kidding?

JAY: I just . . . I don't know what to / . . . say?

THAI: Nothing. You don't have to say anything.

JAY: So if you don't want to get married* / we don't—

THAI: I DON'T—

MUSTARD: *WE DON'T.

JAY: Okay, okay. But should I still come to dinner tomorrow?*

THAI: What?

MUSTARD: *What dinner?

JAY: Like is it still appropriate? For me to meet your parents? / Do they know?

MUSTARD: What dinner?

THAI: Ohmygod, NO, of course they don't / know!

MUSTARD: What dinner?

JAY: Are you going to tell them? Oh god, should we tell them together? Ohmygod. *(matter of fact, cheerful)* This is terrifying. *(then, with genuine fear)* Terrifying.

THAI: You know what else is terrifying? A BABY. Are you going to have a living screaming pooping thing come out of YOUR vagina? / I don't think so!*

MUSTARD: Oh, blecccchhh.

JAY: *Ugcch ucch . . .

THAI: WELL THAT'S WHERE IT COMES OUT OF!

MUSTARD: Stop / stop.

JAY: Wait, it's going to? You're going / to have it?

THAI: I don't know. I DON'T KNOW WHAT I'M / GOING TO DO.

JAY: WE. What WE'RE going to do. Oh, god, oh, god. Okay, we should definitely get married.

MUSTARD / THAI: WHY?

JAY: So the baby has . . . *parents*.

MUSTARD: It *ha*s parents!

JAY: A home. *Love*. You know, / LOVE?

THAI: Where's it gonna live, Jay? In your dorm room?

JAY: No. Of course not, I'll have to leave school!

MUSTARD: It can live with me under the bed if you want.

THAI: Why would you leave school?

JAY: I just . . . that's what people do. Did. In the olden days. / Or whatever.

THAI: Who did? Like in wartime?

MUSTARD: *(stupefied, trying to work through it)* How is a whole baby even going to come out of you—you're so *little*.

THAI: *(to MUSTARD)* It might not.

JAY: Might not what?

THAI: Like, I don't have to have it.*

JAY: What?

MUSTARD: *Of course you have to have it, you stupid idiot, how will it *breathe*?

THAI: We could . . . give it away?

MUSTARD: TO WHO?

JAY: Oh, no. / No, no, no.

THAI: Like, for adoption maybe?

JAY: NO! Ohmygod, no!

THAI: Or I just . . . I don't have to . . . *have it.*

    Beat. This sinks in for JAY.

JAY: But I . . . think I want to have it. I do. I think we want to have it. Don't we?*

THAI: We?

MUSTARD: *Duh.*

JAY: Yeah.

MUSTARD: *It can't just stay in there, swimming around forever!

THAI: I'm saying it could just go . . .

MUSTARD: Where would it go?

THAI: . . . away . . . ?

JAY: NO. No, no, no. I don't want . . . *that.* / I may be old-fashioned, but I don't want *that.**

MUSTARD: Want what? Want what? Want what? Want what?

THAI: *(to JAY)* *It's not your decision! Maybe I want that! Maybe that would be better for *it*!

JAY: HOW? No. No. We're gonna have it, and it can live with my parents. *We* can live with my parents, / and then—

THAI: What century do you live in?

JAY: This one!

THAI: I have shit to do, Jay. With my life!

MUSTARD: RIGHT.

THAI: I'm not ready to be a SAD FUCKING MOM.

MUSTARD: Nuh-uh!

THAI: I'm going to art school, and I'm not going to live with your stupid, boring parents.

JAY: Hey! They're not / boring.

THAI / MUSTARD: Yes they are!

THAI: All they talk about is real estate and where to get good matzo-ball soup.

MUSTARD: Oh, snap!

JAY: Well, at least they're still together!

MUSTARD: Uh-oh.

THAI: Boring people should be married to other boring people so they don't inflict their boringness on the rest of us!

MUSTARD: FUCK YOUR BORING PARENTS.

JAY: Ohmygod. Did you just do this so I'd ask you to marry me?

MUSTARD / THAI: What?

THAI: I DIDN'T DO THIS AT ALL. YOU DID THIS—AND WHY WOULD I WANT TO MARRY YOU! YOU ARE OLD AND BORING AND YOU'RE NEVER GOING TO HAVE A REAL JOB!

MUSTARD: What a poo bum!

JAY: WRITING IS A REAL JOB. YOU'RE THE ONE THAT WANTS TO BE AN ARTIST!

THAI: GET OUT.

JAY: FINE.

MUSTARD: YOU, SIR, ARE AN ASSHOLEBUTTFART . . . *(searching)* POOBAG.

JAY scrambles out the window.

YOU'RE A BAG FOR *POO*.

Beat. THAI is taking her fury out on various items in the room.

(excited again) WE'RE HAVING A BABY?

THAI: *(finally clocking mittens)* WHAT ARE YOU WEARING?

MUSTARD: Nothing, what happened to your face?

THAI: Facebite girl jumped me in the park. So I hit her with a brick.

THAI picks up a belt and beats the floor furiously with it.

MUSTARD: You hit her with a *brick*?

THAI: *(still fuming, punctuating words with hits)* She's going to be fine. I mean she will be. It was a small *brick*, and I didn't hit her that *hard*, she was only out for a few minutes and I think the *hockey stick . . . did more . . . damage . . . anyway*!

Beat.

MUSTARD: You hit her with a *hockey stick*?

THAI: Yeah, a couple of times.

MUSTARD: Before the brick?

THAI: Hockey stick, then brick. *(drops belt)* The brick felt more final.

MUSTARD: Ooookay.

Beat. MUSTARD *throws the belt out the window.*

Since when is Jay coming to dinner?

THAI: He probably won't now. It was for Mom to meet him. I thought it might help her feel more connected, maybe.

MUSTARD: To what?

THAI: Me, reality?*

MUSTARD: Reality?

THAI: *She's just completely losing it. Maybe now's not a good time to see Dad.

MUSTARD: When would she see stupidface Bruce?

THAI: I invited him for dinner too.*

MUSTARD: NO. No, no, no!

THAI: *I thought it would be good for both of them to meet Jay, and they could talk, and she could just . . . sign the papers—like, he's not gonna reconsider, so let's just get it over with so we can all move on!

MUSTARD: Well, I don't think any of that is a good idea, because that's like a . . . feelings ambush, but . . . what should I *wear*?

THAI: I thought . . . it would maybe be better if you didn't come. Like, it's not even happening now / so—

MUSTARD: *(indignation)* Yeah. Okay. / Sure.

THAI: Ohmygod, you'd have been *in* the house! You don't have to be a little bitch about it, it's not even a / thing anymore—

MUSTARD: Yeah, yeah, yeah, no, under the bed and at the dinner table are EXACTLY THE SAME THING. Totally. Whatever, I have nothing to wear anyway, forever.

THAI: Okay, draw your own new clothes then.

MUSTARD: Really? You don't want to?

THAI: You're old enough now to pick out your own clothes. Honestly, I can't be worrying about your *pants* later, when I have a career and a house, and kids / and grandkids—

MUSTARD: Oh yeah, with oldman poobum / Jay . . .

THAI: Wait, do I pass you on to my kids?

MUSTARD: What, like arthritis?

THAI: I just can't be worrying about you . . . until . . . what, the day I die? Are you with me till I *die*?

MUSTARD: I hope so, and I hope you never die and I hope we're together forever!

THAI: But . . . when do you go *away*? *(Beat. She has never asked him this.)* Like . . . when is this over?

MUSTARD: . . . Over?

THAI: I just . . . I feel like it's not normal. For you to still be here.

MUSTARD: You're not a normal Person.

THAI: Well, now I want to be normal, okay?

MUSTARD: Then I'd be in the Boonswallows.

THAI: That sounds cool . . .

MUSTARD: It's NOT. It's *dark*. I'd be there with all the other Boons whose Persons didn't need them anymore. But if you *want* me / to go—

THAI: Mustard, I didn't / *say* that—

   JAY climbs back in the window, out of breath.

MUSTARD: Oh, poop on my face!

THAI: What are you doing?

JAY: I wrote you a poem by accident, when I was walking home.

MUSTARD: *(to JAY)* YOU RUIN EVERYTHING.

THAI: No, I don't / want to—

   JAY stands on a chair, does some bizarre sign language / spoken word performance art to accompany his terrible poem.

JAY: Okay. Here goes.

MUSTARD: What is he doing?

JAY: It's a haiku.

   Beat.

Young love—

MUSTARD: Fuck me.

JAY: *(leaps in, unnerved)* You have an old soul even though
You're two years younger than me.*

MUSTARD: *Two* years?

JAY: *I'm sorry I got you pregnant, and I want to do whatever makes you
happy.
Because I think
I love you.

MUSTARD: Is he having a stroke?

JAY: No, I *know*
I love you.
Because you're smart and you think things about the world
And yes, my parents talk about real estate and soup too much.
But I love you and I hate it when we fight.
Forgive me.
I love you.
I really, *really* do.

> *Beat.*

MUSTARD: FUCK OFF.

THAI: That's not a haiku.

JAY: I know. Sorry.

THAI: It's a pretty shitty piece of poetry no matter how you look at it.

JAY: I know, sorry, somewhere in there it just turned into a stream-of-
consciousness-apology-love-letter-confession.

THAI: Did you think I would say I love you too?

JAY: I don't know. Do you?

MUSTARD: *(scared)* Don't say it.

Beat.

THAI: I don't know. Maybe. Maybe I love you.

MUSTARD: No you don't, take that back!

THAI: *(to MUSTARD)* Go away!

JAY: I just got back . . .

THAI: I don't mean you. I'm glad you came back.

She kisses him. MUSTARD tries to pull her away but she bats at him. THAI and JAY fall back onto the bed.

MUSTARD: You do not *love* him.

JAY: Your mom . . .

THAI: She's not home.

MUSTARD: *(leaving)* Oh gross. I'm gone.

MUSTARD comes downstairs. SADIE comes in, liquor store bags in tow. She sees the papers, opens a new box of wine, pours into a glass that was left in the living room. She sees MUSTARD.

SADIE: Good afternoon. Is Thai home?

There are thumps from THAI's room (maybe JAY kicks over her lamp). SADIE hears it. MUSTARD knocks on THAI's door and coughs to warn THAI and to also mask the sound. THAI and JAY are under the covers.

MUSTARD: Nope. *(coughing uncontrollably)* Your *(cough)* mom is home! *(trying to distract SADIE)* Hey, hey. *(gesturing to magazine)* I have a question: What do men wear? Normal men. Businessmen. Bruce was a businessman, right? Businessman . . . One word or two? / Never mind it's two.

SADIE: Suits. They wear suits.

Sounds or giggles from upstairs. MUSTARD tries to cover them up with his own similar sounds, maybe more coughing.

MUSTARD: Oh, suits! *(coughing to door:)* Maybe stop having the sex! *(to SADIE)* What do they look like, suits?

SADIE: I don't know, you've seen them . . . *(picking up magazine)* Like this. Jackets, pants, ties. Sometimes vests . . .

JAY: *(in the throes of passion)* THAI.

MUSTARD: Tie! Tie! That . . . holds it all together?

Thump. This time SADIE hears it.

SADIE: She *is* home. *(heading upstairs)* THAI?

MUSTARD: *(holding up underwear ad)* Hey, is this a businessman?

She keeps moving.

JAY: Ohhhh.

MUSTARD: *Ohhhhhh*, hey, second question: Should we get a puppy?

SADIE: What? / No.

MUSTARD: Thai really wants one.

SADIE: Well, then Thai and I can talk about it.

She's almost at the door.

THAI?

MUSTARD: *(running to front door)* Come on, let's go for a walk!

SADIE: *(hand on doorknob)* What is wrong with you?

MUSTARD: No no, do not go in there!

Beat. SADIE bursts into THAI's room, surprising JAY and THAI, who are on the bed. Maybe we see JAY's bum briefly before he's able to pull his boxers up. JAY covers himself with pillows back and front. Over the course of the next exchange maybe he loses a pillow out the open window. His pants remain around his ankles until just before his exit.

SADIE: OHMYGOD.

JAY: OHMYGOD. Ohmygod, ohmygod, / ohmygod. *(etc.)*

THAI: MOM!

SADIE: Well, this must be old-man-poo-bum Jay.*

THAI: *(recognizing the phrase)* What?

JAY: *Hello, Mrs. Collins. I'm so so sorry, Thai didn't want you to meet me till tomorrow.

SADIE: Well now I've met ALL of you.

JAY: I'm sorry. I'm so / sorry. Ohmygod.

SADIE: Wait, what's happening tomorrow?

THAI: I invited him to dinner to meet you. And also Dad. / I'm sorry.

SADIE: Your father is coming here?

THAI: Yeah.

SADIE: Tomorrow?

JAY: Yeah, tomorrow.

SADIE: *(to JAY)* Thank you. *(to THAI)* You invited *Bruce*?

THAI: Yeah.

JAY: I'm sorry. I'm so so / sorry.

SADIE: Exactly how old are you, Jay?

JAY: Twenty.

SADIE: Twenty!

THAI: We were just kissing, Mom!

SADIE: Yeah, and I'm made of baby lobsters.*

MUSTARD *giggles because she's quoting him.*

THAI: *(recognizing the phrase again)* What?

JAY: *I know I'm a bit older . . .

SADIE: A bit!

JAY: She's *eighteen.*

THAI: Mom. Don't!

SADIE: She is SIXTEEN, mister. ONE, SIX.

JAY: SIXTEEN? OHMYGOD. *(to THAI)* Why didn't you tell me! / Ohmygod.

SADIE: I should have you arrested!

THAI: MOM!

JAY: Um, you can't cuz this would still be totally legal . . . but *oh god.*

SADIE: She is in HIGH SCHOOL.

JAY: OHMYGOD.

SADIE: I'd like you to leave, Jay. I think that would be appropriate.

JAY: Totally. Of course! *(can't help himself)* . . . But should I still come for dinner tomorrow? It's okay if not, I think I can return the suit. And the flowers.

THAI: You already bought flowers?

JAY: Yeah, I already bought flowers and they died, so I was *obviously* going to buy new flowers, but if I'm not coming I won't!

SADIE: YOU'RE NOT COMING. GET OUT.

JAY looks from SADIE to THAI, hobbles to the door and shuts it so he can pick up his stuff. SADIE tries to come in but he slams the door shut with his bum.

(to MUSTARD, whispered) I'm going to kill you!

MUSTARD: I told you not to go in there!

SADIE makes insane hand gestures meant to mimic his hat.

SADIE: "What do businessmen wear?" "Maybe we should get a puppy."

JAY opens the door and catches SADIE talking to the air. She acts nonchalantly. He hops down the stairs, pants still around his ankles. JAY pulls up his pants and puts on his shoes in the living room before going out the front door. MUSTARD watches him angrily. Finally the door shuts behind him. SADIE goes back into THAI's room. MUSTARD eavesdrops from the living room.

THAI: I have never been so embarrassed in my entire life!

SADIE: What is wrong with you? Fighting, lying about your age, having an older boy upstairs in your room, doing . . . I don't even know! Yes, I do know, I know. Are you even using protection?

THAI: Oh, are you gonna be a mom now? Are we gonna have "the talk"? All you do is sit in the living room drinking and muttering to yourself— I'm legitimately concerned about *your* well-being!

SADIE: Oh, *thank you.*

THAI: I think maybe YOU should be seeing someone, Mom!

SADIE: Maybe I am! Maybe I am SEEING SOMEONE. And never you mind about my well-being—you just concentrate on not being a stereotypical teenage slut!

Beat.

I'm sorry. Thai, sorry. That was . . . completely out of line.

THAI: *(cold, calm)* Isn't that why you married Dad in the first place? Because you were *knocked up*?*

SADIE: Did your father tell you that?

THAI: *And by your definition, that makes you a slut too. And you weren't even *young*, you were just *stupid*, and he probably felt sorry for you. *(beat)* Can you get out of my room now, please. I'm grounded, and I'd like to be alone.

SADIE: You don't have to be / grounded—

THAI: Oh, no, I'm grounding myself, because sluts *should* be grounded, so you go be grounded in your room, and I'll be grounded in my room and / everyone can just—

SADIE: You don't get to ground / yourself!

THAI: THEN GROUND ME ALREADY. DO SOMETHING LIKE AN ACTUAL MOM FOR ONCE IN YOUR LIFE.

SADIE: FINE. YOU'RE GROUNDED. FOREVER. AND SO IS MUSTARD.*

THAI: HE DIDN'T DO ANYTHING.

MUSTARD: *(quietly)* *I didn't do anything.

THAI: Okay, okay, here we go, I'm sorry that someone loves me. I'm sorry that I have my whole life ahead of me, and I AM SO, SO, SO sorry that I'm the only one in this house getting any action!

She slams the door on SADIE, screams into a pillow on her bed. Maybe SADIE screams into something too. Then she sees MUSTARD.

SADIE: Okay. Okay, I'll go out with you! Tonight, why the fuck not. Let's go on a date in the goddamn sky. Pick me up at eight!

She goes into her room and slams the door. MUSTARD is ecstatic. He sees BUG at the front door.

BUG: Knock, knock.

He runs to it, slams and locks it. LESLIE appears from the bathroom.

LESLIE: That isn't very nice.

As if the door had never been locked, BUG storms in. He is considerably more agitated and worked up than last time.

BUG: Hey. Hello AGAIN. How are ya? Still here? Us too. Funny that. You know, Leslie, it feels like we've been up here so long, I'm starting to forget what the dark looks like!

LESLIE: The dark looks like dark, Bug. It's not a thing you can see. It's like steam.

BUG: You can see steam, Leslie.

LESLIE: But not for long.

BUG: No . . . It . . . what's the word?

LESLIE: Evaporates.

BUG: I'm . . . starting to get pretty frustrated, to be honest—

LESLIE: Honesty is the best policy, Bug.

BUG: *(getting angrier)* —because we can't be expected to stay up here forever, telling somewhom the same thing, over and over and over again, tearing off little bits of him to hang off the Tree back home.

LESLIE: That's the definition of crazypeople, isn't it? Doing the same thing over and over again expecting a different outcome.

BUG: Yeah. It is. And we don't want to be seen as crazypeople by everyone back home.

LESLIE: Crazypeople. One word or two? Bug? Crazypeople. Crazy people—

BUG: Crazypeople? One!

MUSTARD: Thai doesn't want me to go! It's not / my fault.

BUG: You had one warning, mister. And then you had two. And then two came and went, *and no one gets three warnings!*

    BUG hits him with a pillow.

THREE WARNINGS IS CRAZYPEOPLE.

LESLIE: BUG. BUG. Get a hold of yourself.

BUG: I'm sorry. I apologize for my outburst.

MUSTARD: It's not my fault her mom can see me!

LESLIE: But she *can see you.*

MUSTARD: But I don't know why!

BUG: And then you made "A Date." FOR SEEING. Two warnings and he makes a date! I'm gonna—

MUSTARD: You can't kill me!

BUG: Yeah, but we could try.

MUSTARD: And you can't take me away; I have to choose to go, or Thai has to stop seeing me, and she still sees me! I know how this works!

BUG: Geez, he knows an awful lot, Leslie, an awful lot.

LESLIE: He does.

BUG: But you know, Leslie, maybe something bad might happen to a friend of his.

LESLIE: A duck friend?

BUG: Sure, a sparkly duck friend might have a . . . quackcident.

LESLIE: That's very good, Bug.

    BUG mimes murdering a duck.

BUG: Quack.

LESLIE: Very good.

BUG: Quack quack.

Beat.

MUSTARD: Duck Duck would . . . understand.

BUG: Oh my.

LESLIE: That's a bit . . . heartless, isn't it?

BUG: You know, I wonder . . .

LESLIE: What?

BUG: Maybe he doesn't have *all* the information.

LESLIE: They never do.

BUG: Think he knows it's going to get worse?

LESLIE: *She's* going to get worse.

MUSTARD: Thai? Why?

LESLIE: Because you've outstayed your welcome.

BUG: Goes from bites in the face, to whacks on the head with hockey sticks, to burying people in cornfields quicker than you might think. That's what happened to that Man's son.

LESLIE: Man's son?

BUG: Man's son.

LESLIE: Oh, Manson. / Manson, Bug.

BUG: Manson. / Manson.

LESLIE: Manson. Yes. He went crazypeople.

BUG: Right, his poor Boon—

LESLIE: Horsefoot.

BUG: Good old Horsefoot—he hung himself off the Tree, di'n't he. Wasn't pretty. We all felt real bad about that. We made a mistake, and we're not making it again. You fool me once, shame on you, but you can't fool two people with one stone—that's a saying.

LESLIE: You see it always ends in tears. And broken necks. And other things. Sticky things.

MUSTARD: Thai would never hurt anyone.

LESLIE: But she is hurting someone. Someones.

BUG: We all have to go home sometime, mister.

MUSTARD: I *am* home. I'm staying for HER. Why don't you understand that?

BUG: But when DO you go away? She did ask him that, didn't she, Leslie?

LESLIE: Very good, Bug.

BUG: *(to LESLIE)* Maybe she's already having trouble seeing him.

LESLIE: Maybe.

BUG: You're like steam, mister. I can see you now.

LESLIE: But not for long.

BUG: You can never be sure when a somewhom's just going to . . . evaporate.

LESLIE: Very good, Bug.

They start to go.

BUG: Catch.

BUG throws MUSTARD a crumpled paper bag. It lands on the floor. They go. MUSTARD looks in the bag. Reaches in. His hand comes out covered in glitter, or holding glittery feathers, or even a full glitter duck head if you just wanna go for it. He almost starts to cry.

MUSTARD: It's not a warning if you've done it already! Oh, Duck Duck.

MUSTARD goes upstairs clutching the bag, distraught. THAI is putting on makeup.

THAI: You look terrible.

MUSTARD: Yeah, maybe if I went away, I wouldn't look so terrible, I wouldn't look anything, because I'd be GONE. And then I wouldn't be your slave anymore.

THAI: Woah. You're so touchy lately, it's like everything I say insults you!

MUSTARD: Maybe that's what happens when you grow up. You start sucking at being nice.

THAI: Then get some new friends.

MUSTARD: I don't want new friends!

THAI: Sorry, I mean, maybe you want to meet new people . . . Maybe you want a girlfriend or . . . a boyfriend.

MUSTARD: No, you're my only Person. We don't get a SPARE.

THAI: Maybe you want to explore a little . . . go somewhere else. You can't live under the bed forever!

MUSTARD: *(vicious)* Why, do you need it for storage?

THAI: No, that's not / what I—

MUSTARD: Do you have some old comics or ice skates you need to get out of the way?

THAI: Aren't you LONELY?

MUSTARD: OF COURSE I'M LONELY. EVERYONE'S LONELY . . . But we all . . . cope. We're all COPING, aren't we?

THAI: But what will you do when I get married?

MUSTARD: To JAY? I just watched you have a huge fight!

THAI: Yeah, couples fight and they make up! Look at Mom and Dad.

MUSTARD: YOUR MOM AND DAD ARE NOT MAKING UP. They are pretty much an example of how *not* to be married because your dad was / a huge loser.

THAI: My dad was a . . . good / dad!

MUSTARD: No, you know what? Your dad, this shining hero of a dad you remember? He was always "working late" and he would come back smelling like . . . like what a cliché probably smells like, and when he was here, he was drinking vodka and picking apart little things you and your mom did, like not closing Tupperware properly, or leaving the remote in the freezer, or not knowing where Cape Breton is. Why don't you remember *those* things?

THAI: My dad fucking LOVED us!

MUSTARD: Well, I'm not very good at English, but I'm pretty sure when you talk about something in the past tense, that means it's *gone*.

THAI punches MUSTARD, hard. He reels.

THAI: Hit me back. If you want.

MUSTARD: *(shocked)* I don't wanna . . . / *hit you.*

THAI: It might . . . help you. It might be fun. Come on, you're the monster under the bed. Go ahead. Hit me.

MUSTARD: I'm not . . . a monster, and I'm not going to *hit you.* This is getting really / scary.

THAI: I just want someone in this house to do SOMETHING. You're my Boon, and you have to do what I say—

MUSTARD: Like a slave? You don't know *anything* about monsters!

THAI: Well you don't know anything about friendship and helping and being a HUMAN BEING!

MUSTARD: I know more than you will ever know about human beings and what they want and need and feel, AND SOMETIMES I WANT SOMETHING FOR ME.

THAI: Yeah, you just want to stay out of the Boonswallows, which I'm starting to think is exactly where you belong.

He hits her, hard. He is shocked he did that, holding back tears.

MUSTARD: That was awful. That was an awful thing to say. And I'm sorry to say it, but it felt good to hit you because what you said was so awful, but now it feels so bad . . . really, really bad.

THAI: I'm going out with Jay, and he's probably going to ask me to marry him again, and you know what, maybe I'll say yes.

She goes out the window. MUSTARD is a wreck. SADIE comes down the hall to THAI's room, maybe with a glass of wine in hand. She knocks on the door.

SADIE: THAI.

MUSTARD: She left.

SADIE: Oh.

MUSTARD: I'm still here though! *(trying to switch gears)* I'm excited!

SADIE: Just so you know, this is going to be the worst date ever.

MUSTARD: Well, I've never been on one before, so it'll be the best one *I've* ever had!

He comes down into the living room, excitedly, assuming that's where the date will be.

SADIE: Okay, I'm going to put on a dress.

MUSTARD: Okay, me too. I'm just kidding!

He grabs the divorce papers and the fashion magazine and returns to THAI's room.

I'll pick you up in ONE MINUTE.

He dives under the bed. Maybe we hear construction sounds starting. From under the bed:

Uh . . . What would Bruce wear on a date? Back when he loved you and wanted to impress you?

SADIE: Oh. Um . . . a suit. A three-piece suit. He had one that was . . . blue. I used to think blue suits were really trashy, but he looked . . . great. I guess you can just wear what you're wearing. Since no one else can see you anyway.

MUSTARD: Ha. Ha.

SADIE: No, it's just . . . I guess you don't have any clothes? Or just the clothes that Thai draws you? I have that old sweater of Bruce's kicking around if you want to wear something more . . . normal?

MUSTARD: No, thank you, I do not want to wear stupidface Bruce's stupid-face sweater. It probably smells like farts!

SADIE: Suit yourself.

MUSTARD: THAT IS WHAT I AM TRYING TO DO!

MUSTARD emerges from under the bed wearing a beautiful, expensive-looking three-piece blue suit that fits him like a glove. It's the kind of old-fashioned suit that hipsters will be rocking forever. Also a tiny briefcase. He straightens his tie, takes off his hat, looks at himself in the mirror. Smooths his hair. He's very pleased. He takes his little briefcase down the hall as if heading to work like a mock grown-up, whistling. He knocks on SADIE's bedroom door. SADIE answers wearing a beautiful red dress. His whistle turns into a pleased, gentle wolf whistle. They take each other in.

SADIE: Oh!

MUSTARD: Wow! You look . . . wow. You look . . . so beautiful.

SADIE: Thank you. You too.

MUSTARD: Do you like the Sometimes Vest?

She gives him a blank look.

My Sometimes Vest? You said . . . you said businessmen . . . they wear jackets, ties and sometimes vests. Did I get it wrong?

SADIE: No. *(beat)* You look perfect.

MUSTARD: Thank you. Oh, I took the liberty of turning something that makes you sad into something that will make you laugh. Hold this.

He gives her the briefcase, pulls out the divorce papers folded into hats. Maybe puts one on.

Ta-da! Divorce hats! One for me *(puts it on)* and one for you!

She puts hers on.

It fits you perfectly.

SADIE: Oh, I have something for you too! Well, for us.

She goes off stage. He pulls out his pocket square, maybe blows his nose, wipes his face, lays it on the coffee table as a tablecloth. He opens his tiny briefcase—inside is a music box, two candles and a small vase with a flower. He opens the music box and it plays a sweet melody.

(off stage) I got it as a gift. I've been saving it. I don't know for what. Honestly, I can't tell the cheap stuff from the good stuff—I think you'll like it though, it's very fizzy!

SADIE re-enters holding a bottle of fancy champagne to the melody of the music box and the tiny date set-up on her coffee table. She is touched.

MUSTARD: I know it's not star flowers, but I didn't have much notice.

SADIE: It's perfect.

SADIE grabs two glasses from the bar, pops the cork—MUSTARD is delighted. She pours, raises her glass to show him what to do.

Cheers.

MUSTARD takes a sip and spits some up, or just opens his mouth and lets it run out—he is not a fan. SADIE is not looking, so he pours the rest of his glass quickly over his shoulder onto the floor. She notices his glass is empty, thinks he enjoyed it and refills it immediately, to his despair.

MUSTARD: Hey, I hope you're hungry.

He produces a package of Pop Rocks.

SADIE: What is that?

MUSTARD: The most amazing food ever invented . . . Pop Rocks! They pop and fizz. *Inside your mouth.* They are just DELIGHTFUL. Go on, try them.

He looks at the champagne, pours them into their glasses to improve the flavour. They fizz loudly—it's magical.

Now tell me you don't believe in magic.

Beat.

SADIE: You know . . . you don't have to prove that magic is real. I'm here. I'm having a nice time.

MUSTARD: Me too.

They try the Pop Rocks champagne. It is truly terrible.

(to himself) So. Much. Worse. *(awkward beat, then, cheerfully)* So why do you think Bruce left?

SADIE: That's not the kind of thing you're supposed to say on a date.

MUSTARD: Oh. Sorry. I was just trying to make conversation.

SADIE: He left because he fell out of love with me.

MUSTARD: How?

SADIE: I don't know, I'm not out of it. I still wake up hoping that it's all a dream and he's still snoring peacefully beside me. Bruce was very warm— he radiated heat. Now I wake up cold.

Beat.

MUSTARD: Is *that* the kind of thing you're supposed to say on a date?

SADIE: Oh god, no. Sorry. When you break up with someone without closure, you just feel like you have all these things to say to them. And you can't.

MUSTARD: You can say them to me.

SADIE: It's not the same.

MUSTARD: I mean you do it already, don't you? You do it all the time, don't you? You talk to him like he's here, and I'm here, so talk to me. For closure. You said I looked like him.

SADIE: You . . . do. Even more now. It's uncanny.

MUSTARD: You said he had a blue suit.

SADIE: . . . he did.

MUSTARD: Okay.

He takes his divorce hat off, smooths his hair.

There. I'm Bruce. I'm Bruce.

SADIE: This is so fucked up. You're okay with this?

MUSTARD: Totally. It'll be fun.

He seems to morph over the next exchange—becoming more serious, more like a real person when he is pretending to be BRUCE, like he's somehow taken a MasterClass in BRUCE acting.

(as BRUCE) Hello.

He kisses her hand.

Hello, loml.

SADIE: What?

MUSTARD: *(as MUSTARD)* That's what he called you, right? Love of my life? L-O-M-L. Loml. I used to think he was saying "lama," then I figured it out. Say hello back. It's rude not to.

SADIE: Hello. Loml.

MUSTARD: *(as MUSTARD)* I hear you have some things to say to me.

SADIE: No, he . . . he wouldn't say that.

MUSTARD: Well what would he say? I've never been a husband before.

SADIE: He'd say . . . I'm all ears, kiddo.

Beat.

MUSTARD: *(as BRUCE)* I'm all ears, kiddo. *(as MUSTARD)* Come on, it'll be fun, give it a try!

Beat.

SADIE: *(deep breath, eyes closed)* There is a man on the radio that sounds like you.

MUSTARD: *(as BRUCE)* You're doing great, kiddo. But you gotta open your eyes. Look at me.

She does.

Say my name.

SADIE: *(relieved somehow)* Bruce.

MUSTARD: *(as BRUCE)* That's me.

SADIE: There is a man on the radio that sounds like you. And sometimes when I'm driving, I turn the volume up all the way, so that his voice fills up the whole car until I can feel it in my bones. And that makes me feel like . . . you're there.

MUSTARD: *(as BRUCE)* I wish I could be there, kiddo. I really do. Look at me. Say my name.

SADIE: Bruce. Oh, Bruce, I heard this terrible joke the other day—

MUSTARD: *(as BRUCE)* What was it?

SADIE: What do you call a can opener that doesn't work?

MUSTARD: *(as BRUCE)* What?

SADIE: A *can't* opener.

MUSTARD: *(as MUSTARD, losing it, slapping his knee)* A CAN'T OPENER. *(as BRUCE)* That's really / funny, Sades.

SADIE: Awful! I knew you'd love it. It's awful, and it's not funny, and all I could think was how much I wanted to tell it to you, because you love jokes like that.

MUSTARD: *(as BRUCE)* It's a great joke, kiddo. Okay, don't stop, what else you got? Get it all out.

SADIE: *(almost crying)* And I'm so worried about Thai. I'm worried. I drink too much and I take pills and it's not just because you left, it's because I have no idea how not to fuck her up because I imagined it would so much easier than it actually is—

MUSTARD: *(as BRUCE)* What?

SADIE: *Being a parent.* And I thought we were going to do it together.

MUSTARD: *(maybe holding her, as BRUCE)* I'm sorry, loml. I'm so / so sorry.

SADIE: Don't . . . say that. You don't get to call me that anymore!

MUSTARD: *(as BRUCE)* I'm upsetting you.

SADIE: Oh, OH, and I'm seeing her imaginary friend, Mustard, remember him? As a matter of fact, we're on a date! Hah! Right now! Mustard and I are on a DATE. Because I'm so desperate for affection that I'll agree to anything because I still fucking love you. I can't help it. You don't stop loving someone because they stop loving you.

MUSTARD: *(as BRUCE)* You don't have to.

He goes to kiss her.

SADIE: Oh god, is this real? Are you here?

MUSTARD: *(as BRUCE)* Does it matter? Sades. LOML. I love you. I still love you.

They almost kiss.

SADIE: Woah! No, no, stop being Bruce.

She moves away from him.

MUSTARD: *(as MUSTARD)* Why, I thought I was doing a great job! I love you! I love you! I love / you!

SADIE: You're just saying that because you think that that's what you're supposed to say on a date. And you think you're supposed to kiss me! You think you're supposed to fall in love!

MUSTARD: Well what are dates for if not to fall in love? What am I supposed to say?

SADIE: Small talk! What we do, our favourite foods! We just . . . figure one another out.

MUSTARD: But I've figured you out. I know you, and I love you! For real!

SADIE: No, you / don't.

MUSTARD: YES I DO. Why does this have to be so fucking confusing! I love you!

SADIE: WHY?

MUSTARD: WHY DO YOU NEED A REASON? I KNOW THAT I LOVE YOU BECAUSE I LOVE YOU. I bet you miss kissing.

SADIE: I miss a lot of things.

MUSTARD: Okay, so would you . . . maybe like to kiss me? Or I could kiss you. I have lips.

Beat.

SADIE: Can you even do that?

Beat.

MUSTARD: Why, do you think I'll evaporate or something? Fizz away like Pop Rocks?

SADIE: No . . .

MUSTARD: Why would you even go on a date with me if you thought I couldn't kiss you?

SADIE: No. I don't know. This is the weirdest date I've ever been on. If I'm actually on it.

MUSTARD: Just stop it! Either you see me or you don't. Either I'm real or I'm not. I can't sit here drinking bubbly water and eating Pop Rocks with someone who doesn't believe in me, that's crazypeople!

SADIE: I'm sorry / I didn't mean—

MUSTARD: You know why you can see me? You know why all this is happening? Why I'm missing teeth and fingernails and Duck Duck is missing a whole HEAD?*

SADIE: A head?

MUSTARD: *Because maybe you needed a *friend*. Because you were sad, and lonely, and you needed someone to care about you or you were going to kill yourself! You pineneedle and pineneedle after Bruce, and he doesn't love you anymore, and I do, and I'm *right here*. A bird in the hand flies away if you don't feed it!

SADIE: What?

MUSTARD: IT'S A SAYING. Everyone wants to grow up and forget about us and magic and fucking *whimsy*, and have *babies* and *husbands* and *(spits it) jobs* and be miserable poopy adults that don't even try to see us when we come back to visit, and you don't ever for a second think of how much danger I might be in, or what it's like to be left alone in the house, under the bed—it is TERRIFYING—*

SADIE: I never knew that—

MUSTARD: *Or how it might be nice for me to see what a kiss feels like! And I'm sorry I don't understand your stupid poopy language. I'm sorry I live under the bed, and I'm sorry I love you because you need to be loved, no, you *deserve* to be loved. But I deserve to be loved too. I need to be needed. I think it should be enough to love someone, and you shouldn't have to explain it. Not everything has to have an explanation. Explain cold fusion, explain the placebo effect, EXPLAIN RAINBOWS.

She kisses him. MUSTARD beams.

SADIE: Actually, you can explain rainbows, / it's a reflection—

He kisses her again. It's that first kiss from grade five—no technique, but full marks for enthusiasm.

MUSTARD: Oh, geez. Wow. That is, that is so nice. Can I . . . can we go again? Let's go again.

He does. He is learning the art of kissing very quickly. SADIE is wobbly, bashful. Maybe she leans her head on his shoulder. Beat.

So . . . Do we have the sex now? And then you get pregnant, and then we get married, and then we get divorced?

SADIE: What? No! I mean, I don't know. *(laughs)* This is all moving pretty quick.

MUSTARD: No it's not. I've loved you forever and ever, and we only *just* had our first kiss.

SADIE: I can't promise anything, but we can lie in bed in our PJs and drink the rest of this bubbly water and make small talk. And maybe . . . kiss some more. If you'd like.

MUSTARD: Wow. That would be just so great.

She starts to go.

Oh, wait!

MUSTARD throws his suit jacket on the ground over where he spilled the champagne earlier.

Milady. So you don't get your feet wet.

SADIE: You are a strange and special man.

MUSTARD: *(beaming)* Thank you for calling me a man.

MUSTARD sees LESLIE at the window.

I'll be right there.

SADIE goes, taking the champagne with her. He runs to the window and locks it. As if it had never been locked, LESLIE opens the window. He is angry, but it is a terrifying, quiet anger.

LESLIE: Naughty. Very, very naughty.

The door opens and THAI comes in, pretty distraught. She's been crying. She runs into a hug with MUSTARD. LESLIE slinks away.

THAI: *(pulling back)* Woah— What are you wearing?

MUSTARD: Do you like it?

THAI: Yeah. A lot.

MUSTARD goes over to the window and locks it again. Notices THAI's face.

MUSTARD: What's wrong?

THAI: I hurt Jay. I mean I think I really hurt him.

MUSTARD: *(a little too hopeful)* Did you guys break up?

THAI: No. I . . . I smashed a glass on his head. Some of it went in his eye . . .

MUSTARD: You smashed glass in his . . . / eye.

THAI: He took me to a really nice restaurant, and he proposed again, but this time he had a ring baked into the dinner roll. He had to, like, force me to break it open, because I didn't want any bread. And then—I don't know why . . . I just got . . . so . . . *angry*.

MUSTARD: So you smashed a glass in his *eye*?

THAI: No, on his *head*. He was bleeding so much and he was screaming and screaming, and then . . . he went to the hospital and I ran home, but I'm still so . . . *angry*. Maybe it is the baby, but it's freaking me out. What's wrong with me?

MUSTARD: You hit me too.

THAI: *(vicious)* You deserved it! Sorry. I just don't know how I'm supposed to treat you now that I'm older.

MUSTARD: Well, you're not supposed to hit me. Just treat me the same!

THAI: But things can't stay the same forever. *I'm different*, we can't just hide in the closet all afternoon and eat Pop Rocks. I don't even like Pop Rocks anymore.

MUSTARD: You shut your dumb face.

THAI: I know you're afraid of the Boonswallows, but maybe they're not that bad. What if they're different for everyone? You can't be afraid of something you've never experienced . . .

MUSTARD: You're afraid of the baby.

Beat.

THAI: Can you visit? Maybe you can visit.

MUSTARD: You wouldn't see me. If I came back.

THAI: I'd see you. I'd always see you.

MUSTARD: I mean, I know / you would try . . .

THAI: I'd see you. I'd see you.

MUSTARD: If you want me to go, I'll go. I'll go right now. You just have to decide to stop seeing me, and that'll be that.

Beat. This sinks in. THAI suddenly sees the remains of the date.

THAI: Ummm . . . Ohmygod! Am I interrupting something? Do you have a special friend I don't know about?

MUSTARD: No.

THAI: Is there someone here?

She swipes the air around the date set-up with her hand.

Is it someone else's Boon? That kid's down the street? I thought you said that Boon looked like a Transformer!

MUSTARD: No, no, it isn't! / It's not. It's not.

THAI: Mustard! This is awesome! You're on a date! What's she wearing? / Or he?

MUSTARD: Nothing / because—

THAI: NOTHING? / Whoooo!

MUSTARD: No, no! Because she's not there! There is no her! *(more from THAI)* Okay, she's naked and she just left!

THAI: Oooh. I knew it! Okay, so just clean up so Mom doesn't get weirded out in the morning. And then . . . *(starts heading upstairs)* will you come upstairs and tell me a story? Until I fall asleep?

>MUSTARD *is touched.* LESLIE *pokes his head out of the bathroom door.* BUG *appears somewhere else. They listen for* MUSTARD's *answer.*

MUSTARD: I would be truly honoured to tell you a story.

>THAI *goes into her room.*

BUG: *(like a buzzer)* ENNNNN!!!

LESLIE: Wrong answer.

>BUG *storms into the living room, grabs* MUSTARD.

BUG: Okay, mister, I've had it with you—*

MUSTARD: No, you heard her!

BUG: *I don't care what the rules say—*

LESLIE: Thank you, Bug—

BUG: *I'm going to rip out your / insides—*

LESLIE: That's enough, Bug—

MUSTARD: You saw! You saw!

LESLIE: Sit down, Bug.

BUG: *—and shove them up your backside until / they come out—

MUSTARD: She *wants* me to stay.

BUG throws MUSTARD over an armchair, is about to strangle him.

LESLIE: SIT DOWN, BUG.

BUG does.

MUSTARD: I'm *sorry*—

LESLIE: Shh.

MUSTARD: She *asked*—

LESLIE: Shh. Hush your mouth. Bug is very talented with pain—

BUG: Thank you, Leslie.

LESLIE: —but sometimes words hurt best, so I'll use a few of them now. Here is one word, or rather, a name: Wembley. Have you heard of her?

MUSTARD: No.

LESLIE: Wembley was like you—her story was like yours. Wembley stayed with her Person, let's call him—

BUG: Robbie.

LESLIE: —Robbie, for many years longer than advised. And because she had so much time in the light, Wembley succeeded in appearing to Robbie's father, let's call him—

BUG: Old Robbie.

LESLIE:—Robbie the *Older*, who needed to fall in love—so he fell. Falling is the easy part. Isn't it?

MUSTARD: You've never been in love.

LESLIE: I have.

BUG: *(wry)* Huh.

LESLIE: Bug has. We both have.

   Beat.

So Wembley married Robbie the Older.

MUSTARD: *(in awe)* Can we do that?

BUG: JUST LISTEN.

LESLIE: Bug and I did everything we could to convince her to come back, but she was very strong, and her bond with the two Robbies was very strong, and for a time everything was beautiful, and we began to wonder, not without hope, if we'd been wrong about how the world could be. Bug in particular was very excited about the possibilities. He's more sensitive than you might think. It hurts him to hurt you.

BUG: It hurts.

LESLIE: But then, almost without warning, Child Robbie became angry and violent, and something ugly rotted away at his insides, and he began to do excruciating things to the people and animals that he met.

BUG: Horrible. / Horrible.

LESLIE: But by the time Wembley realized the mistake she had made, it was too late—Robbie had become something altogether different, and, one day, this new thing that had been Child Robbie opened its mouth and devoured its father, Robbie the Older, with its teeth, which were now sharp and large, then it smelled out Wembley with its long snout, and ran to her on its hooves, and tore her into small and perfect pieces with its claws, and sucked on her bones with its sandpaper tongue. Then it caught fire and burnt into ashes and scattered itself to the wind.

Beat.

And *that* is how it goes. That is how it *will* go.

MUSTARD: How is that . . . *possible?*

LESLIE: The world is mysterious.

Beat.

MUSTARD: Is that real? Is that a real story?

LESLIE: Saying something makes it real.

MUSTARD: But is it true?

LESLIE: It is true for the moment.

MUSTARD: . . . No, no, no, this is another warning.

LESLIE: There are no more warnings. These are just words. Nothing more. And words hurt. But teeth, and claws and nails are stronger than words. And sharper.

Beat.

And that is the end.

BUG: The. End.

MUSTARD: No, no, no. There was never a Boon named Wembley.

LESLIE: Names are just words, after all.

BUG: Sometimes we mix 'em up.

Beat.

LESLIE: Go on. She's waiting for you. Tell her a story.

BUG: Make it a good one.

LESLIE: But make it the *last one*. Not for me, not for Bug, but for her.

LESLIE and BUG go. MUSTARD goes to THAI's room. Maybe he brings the music box. THAI is already in bed, dozing. MUSTARD tucks her in. He sits beside her. She snuggles against him. He opens the music box, lets the music play.

MUSTARD: Here's one you haven't heard before. Once upon a time there was a perfect little girl. And she had a very funny, very handsome best friend and they were together all the time. But then one day, when she was playing with her dad, she cut her knee. But instead of crying out for her dad, she cried out for her best friend, and that made her dad really angry, and he said that her friend had to go away. And he did. He started to . . . But then he realized he forgot his favourite hat, so he came back, and the dad was . . . gone—well he was there, but he wasn't, and that little girl was all alone, and the best friend promised he would never ever ever leave her alone until he was sure she didn't need him anymore. And now . . . he doesn't know.

He stops the music.

He just doesn't know.

Beat.

Are you asleep? Say something.

Beat. MUSTARD *gets up and smooths the covers over* THAI, *looks at her sadly.*

(whispered) The story's about us, you know.

He turns the lights off in her room. Time passes. It is Friday. SADIE *paces, cleans nervously. There's a knock at the door. She opens it to reveal* JAY, *in an ill-fitting suit, his eye covered with a patch (due to the glass-in-the-eye situation), with a comically large bouquet of fake flowers and a box of chocolates.* SADIE *smooths her hair, then opens the door.*

JAY: *(very official)* Hello, Mrs. Collins.

SADIE: It's Fray. / What are you doing here?

JAY: Mrs. / Fray. Right. Sorry.

SADIE: Ms. / Ms.

JAY: Ms. Ms.

SADIE: Oh! What happened to your eye?

JAY: I slipped in the shower.

SADIE: I thought I told you not to come / tonight.

JAY: Yes, you did, sorry, but I felt it was important to meet Mr. Fray.

SADIE: No, *he's* Collins, / because that's *his* name.

JAY: Oh. Right. Sorry. I know I made a bad impression last time I was here.

SADIE: You did, and you weren't supposed / to come—

JAY: Please. I'm an honourable . . . boy . . . man. *(now with certainty)* Man. And I've come to do a brave thing.

THAI comes downstairs, dressed nicely.

THAI: What brave thing.

JAY reveals flowers to both women.

JAY: Miladies.

SADIE: Jesus Christ, are these fake?

JAY: Yeah, so they / won't die—

THAI: I told you not to come.

SADIE: *(to THAI)* Your father will be / here any minute!

THAI: Mom, I'm sorry, I didn't think / he'd come.

SADIE: It's fine, he might as well stay now that he's here.

THAI: I don't think it's a good / idea.*

SADIE: Bruce is late. Of course.

SADIE *goes off stage to get a vase.*

JAY: *It's the best idea. It's the only idea.

THAI: Why are you here?

JAY: Oh, I wanted to make a grand gesture.

THAI: I don't like chocolate.

JAY: What? Oh. / Shit.

SADIE: *(off stage)* Shit. Thai, can you run to the corner store and grab some cranberry juice for your dad's vodka?

SADIE *comes back on, grabs money from her purse, gives it to* THAI.

THAI: He can just use orange juice.

SADIE: THAI. PLEASE.

THAI: Fine. Come on, Jay.

JAY: I'm fine. I'll just stay here. With your mom.

Beat.

THAI: *(suspicious)* Okay . . . I'll be right back. Just don't . . . do or say anything at all.

She goes.

JAY: Are you all right?

SADIE: I'm just a bit nervous. I haven't seen Bruce in a while. Try to laugh at his terrible jokes.

JAY: Right. *(to himself)* Laugh at his jokes. I will. / Definitely—

SADIE: Or maybe he won't make jokes. It's not like this is a social call—he's just coming to get the papers. Oh Jesus, the papers. Where did I put them?

She searches. A knock on the door.

Oh god, that's him.

SADIE opens it to reveal BRUCE, who is, of course, played by the same actor playing MUSTARD, only this time there is no wavering. He is a different person, a real man. He comes in. It is awkward.

BRUCE: Hey, kiddo. *(awkward beat)* You look really good. *(notices her staring)* What?

SADIE: Nothing, nothing. You're just . . .

BRUCE: You're staring.

SADIE: Sorry . . . you just look like someone I know.

BRUCE: I am someone you know.

SADIE: Right. / Right.

BRUCE: Hey, did you cook? It smells amazing in here.

SADIE: Yes, but it's not a big / deal . . .

BRUCE: Sades! That is . . . that is *really* big of you. I really do miss your cooking. Jessica thinks Kraft Dinner is gourmet dining.

JAY laughs too loudly at what he thinks is a joke. BRUCE finally notices him.

Ah, this must be the older boyfriend. Nice eye patch! *(like a pirate)* Yarrr!

JAY: Yarrr!

BRUCE: Hey, why don't pirates go to strip clubs?

JAY: Why?

BRUCE: They already have all the booty!

JAY laughs, too loudly.

Yeah . . . So. You're in college, right?

JAY: Yes, sir.

BRUCE: What are you studying?

JAY: English literature. I do very well. I get all high *seas* . . . Yarrr.

Epic. Joke. Fail.

BRUCE: Oh, yeah, that's another pirate joke . . . yeah. Okay, okay. English lit—maybe you can help me out with something there, teach. I was just having this argument with someone at work. A lot. Allot. One word or two?*

SADIE: What? *(beat)* What?

JAY: *Well, sir, it can be both, actually. "A lot" refers to an amount, but if you add an "l," it refers to a distribution of* a quantity.

SADIE: *(quietly, to BRUCE, meaning MUSTARD)* Ohmygod, it's you. It *is* you.

BRUCE: *But alot with one "l"—that's not a word?

JAY: No.

SADIE: *(to BRUCE, almost whispered)* What are you doing here?*

BRUCE: *(to SADIE)* What?

JAY: *It's a common mistake—but it actually doesn't exist.

SADIE: *(to BRUCE)* NO, you don't.

JAY: It doesn't really matter.

BRUCE: *(to JAY)* I'm sorry, I didn't say my name, I'm Bruce.*

JAY: Hi, I'm Jay.

SADIE: *Stop it. Stop.

BRUCE: Stop what?

SADIE: Pretending to be him.*

JAY: Jay. Jay. Jay—

BRUCE: *WHO?*

SADIE: Okay. Okay. Fine. We'll do this your way.

JAY: *Jay. Jay!

BRUCE: My way?

JAY: I'M JAY—

BRUCE: YES, THANK YOU, JAY. I HEARD YOU THE FIRST TIME. I'M BRUCE.

SADIE: NO YOU ARE NOT.

Beat. BRUCE *looks at her like she's insane.*

When Thai gets back *she's* going to know it's you and this whole disgusting game is going to be over.*

BRUCE: It's not a game . . .

JAY: *What game?

SADIE: Or maybe this has all been some elaborate trick / to mock the SADDEST SAD!

JAY: What game? What game?

THAI *comes back in, hugs* BRUCE.

THAI: Hi, Daddy.

BRUCE: Hi, kiddo! You look great.

THAI: Thanks, Daddy. How's it going?

BRUCE: Well, good old Jay here looks like he's going to pass out.

THAI: Oh, he's okay. / He's okay.

JAY: I'm okay. Chocolate? Anyone?

SADIE / THAI / BRUCE: No.

SADIE: Bruce? Drink?

BRUCE: No. I stopped drinking.

SADIE: You stopped drinking?

JAY: I'd take a drink . . . May I have a drink please?*

BRUCE: Sure—

THAI: *No. Jay. I still don't get why / you're even here.

JAY: *(cheerful)* Okay. *(to BRUCE)* Have a chocolate, sir. Let's all / have one.

THAI: It's okay, Daddy, you can have a drink.

BRUCE: No, I'm really not drinking anymore.

SADIE: At all?

BRUCE: You should try it, Sades, changes the way you see things.

SADIE: Oh I see things. I *see* things.

THAI: I'll get you a pop.

SADIE: No, no, no, no, no, no. Nobody move.

BRUCE: Nobody move or the girl gets it.

JAY laughs too loudly.

SADIE: What are you trying to do here?

BRUCE: Me? Nothing at all. My daughter invited me to meet her boyfriend, so I came!

SADIE: I thought you came for the papers.

BRUCE: Well, if you have them, and they're ready to go, I can take them, that'd be great, but, it's not a big deal if you need more time.

SADIE: Oh, that's really big of you, Bruce.

JAY: May I have a drink please?*

BRUCE: Sure.

THAI / SADIE: *No.

THAI: I'll get you a pop too.

SADIE: No, no, no, don't you leave me alone with him!

BRUCE: Who?

JAY: I'm not going to hurt you, Mrs. Collins. Here / have a chocolate—

SADIE: FRAY! Ms. Fray.

BRUCE: Fray already, huh?

THAI: Dad.

BRUCE: I'm just kidding.

   JAY laughs too loudly.

Jessica says she doesn't want to take my name anyway.

SADIE: You're getting married?

BRUCE: No, I mean . . .

SADIE: You're getting *married*!

BRUCE: No. I mean, eventually.

JAY: Mazel tov!

BRUCE: *Eventually.*

THAI: Have some wine, Mom.

SADIE: *(to THAI)* Did you know he was getting married?

BRUCE: We're not getting married.

THAI: Yeah, you might, / it's been discussed.

BRUCE: Thai!

SADIE: *We're* still married.

BRUCE: Because you won't sign the papers!

SADIE: Hah! I knew it!

BRUCE: So where are they?

JAY: Will someone have a chocolate?*

THAI: NO.

SADIE: *Divorce hats! Remember? *(aside to THAI)* Did you tell him to come? To fuck with me?

JAY: *(quietly, to THAI)* Is she all right?

THAI: *(to SADIE)* What are you talking about?

SADIE: He looks EXACTLY like him now. EXACTLY. Without that hat, and in those clothes, you look EXACTLY like him. *(to BRUCE)* You look exactly like . . . *you*, but YOU never came upstairs last night, YOU never came upstairs to have THE SEX. SO LET'S JUST ALL SIT THE FUCK DOWN, SHALL WE.

> *Everyone sits, slowly and awkwardly. JAY and THAI sit on the otto-man. JAY falls off. Beat. He stands up, with pomp and circumstance: announcement time.*

JAY: Mr. and Mrs. Collins and Fray . . .

> *THAI keeps trying to pull him down.*

THAI: No! No, no.

JAY: Yes.

THAI: Jay, no!

JAY: YES.

THAI: *(desperate subject change)* What's for dinner?

SADIE: Pop Rocks.

BRUCE / THAI: What?

SADIE: *(defiant)* Chicken.

JAY: Mr. and Mrs. Fray and Collins, / I would like to declare my intentions towards your daughter.* Please.

THAI: No. No!

JAY: Yes!

BRUCE: *Yes, yes, by all means, Jay, declare away. What are your intentions towards my daughter?

SADIE: She's *my* daughter. She's your *PERSON*.

JAY: I've brought these chocolates for everyone to eat, / so if someone could just—

THAI: OHMYGOD, JAY, NOBODY WANTS A CHOCOLATE.

SADIE: CAN YOU FLY, BRUCE?

BRUCE: Are you having a stroke?

SADIE: Can you turn flowers into *stars*?!

BRUCE: *Stars?*

SADIE: All right, I am going to go upstairs to look under the bed / for you.

THAI: Under the bed?

SADIE: And if you're not there . . . I'll know you're you.

She goes upstairs to THAI's room. Everyone follows.

JAY: *(quietly)* Will somebody *please* just have a chocolate.

BRUCE: Yes, Jay, I'll have a goddamn chocolate.

He takes one. SADIE's checking under the bed.

JAY: NOT THAT ONE. HAVE THIS ONE.

BRUCE takes the offered chocolate. Beat.

THAI: Mom. Are you talking / about Mustard?*

JAY: *(quietly, to himself, under everything else)* I intend to marry her, I intend to marry her . . . *(etc.)*

BRUCE: *(to THAI)* *Your imaginary friend Mustard?

THAI: *(to SADIE)* Do you mean Mustard?

BRUCE: From when you were a kid?

THAI: *(to SADIE)* Can you see him? Do you see him / too?

BRUCE bites into the chocolate.

BRUCE: Owwww, what the / fuck—what is this?

BRUCE pulls a ring out of the chocolate.

JAY: I INTEND TO MARRY HER.

THAI: OHMYGOD. / JAY.

JAY takes the chocolate-covered ring from BRUCE, shakes it off, tries to appear more official.

JAY: Mr. and Mrs. / Collins and Fray . . .

THAI: Argh!

JAY: I love your daughter and I intend to / marry her—*

THAI: NO. No. No. *(etc.)*

JAY: *But I wanted your blessing, so I had that ring cooked into a chocolate as a grand gesture, / so that—

THAI: Why would you give it to HIM?

JAY: Because you don't like chocolate!

BRUCE: I could have choked!

SADIE: You can't get *married*.

THAI: We're not going to!

JAY: I just want to do the RIGHT THING here!*

THAI: JAY.

BRUCE: *What the fuck is going / on—

THAI: *(scary, don't mess with her)* JAY.

JAY: I'M JUST TRYING TO MAKE AN HONEST WOMAN OF YOU.

Awkward beat. The cat's out of the bag.

SADIE: Oh my god!

BRUCE: *(to JAY)* I'm going to fucking kill you.

THAI: Daddy . . .

BRUCE charges at JAY. They fight. BRUCE lands some punches. JAY mostly tries to stay out of the way.

Daddy, stop! / It's not his fault!

SADIE: Bruce, stop it!

JAY: We didn't think she'd get pregnant!

BRUCE: Of course you didn't think she'd get pregnant: that's how it works!

JAY: We always used condoms!*

THAI: JAY!

BRUCE: *YOU SON OF A BITCH.

JAY: I DON'T WANT TO HIT YOU, MR. FRAY!

BRUCE: IT'S COLLINS, GODDAMMIT!

BRUCE goes to punch JAY, but JAY ducks and he hits SADIE. She reels.

Sorry! Sades, I'm so sorry! Fuck.

THAI grabs the vase, dumps the flowers, smashes the vase over BRUCE's head. The vase shatters.

THAI.

Beat. BRUCE is in pain, shocked.

THAI: Get out. / GET OUT.

BRUCE: Honey! I was trying to hit *him*.

THAI: GET OUT! Go!

Beat. BRUCE *tries to regroup.*

BRUCE: Thai, none of this is your fault.

THAI: What isn't? Getting pregnant? Because I did that. I was there. That's my fault.

JAY: And mine. I'm so, so sorry.

BRUCE: No, your mother . . . she should have . . . prevented you / from—

THAI: From what?

BRUCE: She should have *protected* you—

THAI: How?

BRUCE: She should have been raising you differently!

THAI: *How?*

BRUCE: Better!

THAI: Well, where the fuck have you been, *Bruce?*

BRUCE: I don't live here anymore!

THAI: Exactly! Even when you lived with us you were never here. I assume you were out fucking the orthodontist.

BRUCE: Hey!

THAI: Maybe I get my slutty behaviour from you.

BRUCE: Help me out here, Sades, would you?

SADIE just glares at him.

Jesus! I'm sorry I stopped drinking, okay? I'm sorry you have to change your name. I'm sorry I fell in love! This is not over, Thai—we are going to talk about this. No daughter of mine / will—

THAI: When I want to see you, I'll call you. Now go.

Beat.

BRUCE: Yeah. Okay.

He tries to hug THAI. She dodges him.

Can I have the papers, Sadie? Where are the papers?

SADIE gets up and brings him the divorce hats, defiantly.

Oh, that's nice. Real nice. Very grown up.

She unfolds them with a pointed look. She signs, hands him his copy. Maybe she puts her divorce hat on again.

SADIE: Now go.

BRUCE: Hey, you know what? Mustard? *(vicious)* Mustard was a *joke.* Mustard was *my* joke, that I made up to make you laugh because you wouldn't stop crying and your mother didn't know what to do with you, so I'd put on a stupid hat and a funny voice, and make silly faces, and you LOVED IT, so don't you talk to me about shitty parenting, because your mother didn't even want you in the first place.

BRUCE leaves. Long beat.

SADIE: Thai . . .

THAI: It's fine. I'm fine. Maybe you should go, Jay.

JAY: Yeah. I get it.

He offers to shake THAI's hand.

Goodbye, goodbye forever.

THAI: What? No, no, just for . . . just for right now. God, you're so dramatic. Here, take your chocolates. Please, just go.

He takes the chocolates, starts to go, sadly.

(reconsidering) Actually . . .

JAY's back in a flash.

I'll keep them. *(earnest)* Thank you.

He's not leaving.

Goodbye.

THAI shuts the door on a hopeful JAY. She tentatively offers the box to SADIE—a peace offering. They sit on the couch, chewing. THAI examines the ring, which was left in the chocolate box. Beat.

SADIE: Thai . . . what he said . . . your father . . .

THAI: It's fine. It's *fine. (beat)* There was nothing you could have done. Just so you . . . like it's not your fault—we were careful—it was just a fluke, I guess. Like I was.

SADIE: Thai . . .

THAI: No, it's okay . . . I don't know if I want to marry Jay . . . Or have a baby with him right now.

SADIE: You don't have to do either. And I will support whatever you choose.

THAI: I know that, but if I were to have it . . . Maybe it's enough for the parents to just love the baby . . . and not each other? And I kind of like the idea of having a thing that *has* to love me.

SADIE: It doesn't have to. You have to help it. I love you though, even when you don't love me. We will figure it out. Face biter. Baby maker. My love is gonna bear hug you until the day you die.

SADIE holds her. Beat.

THAI: Is there chicken?

MUSTARD pushes the tiny briefcase out from under the bed.

SADIE: Oh, there's chicken.

MUSTARD emerges from under the bed, picks up the briefcase. He's trying to keep it together.

THAI: Okay, I'm gonna make a sandwich. I'm starving.

THAI goes off stage to the kitchen. MUSTARD comes out of THAI's room, sees SADIE.

SADIE: Hi.

MUSTARD: Hi.

SADIE: What are you doing?

MUSTARD: Oh, I'm just going out for a bit.

SADIE: For how long?

MUSTARD: . . . Forever, actually.

SADIE: To . . . the Boonswallows?

He nods. Beat. This sinks in.

Okay, no, no, wait a minute.

*She runs off, grabs a massive antique flashlight, hands it to him
sheepishly.*

You said it was dark. It's Bruce's favourite, but, you know. Fuck him.

MUSTARD: Wow. Thank you . . . very very so much. And thank you for
kissing me.

SADIE: My pleasure. *(Beat. She realizes it actually was.)* So . . . Do you . . .
vanish . . . now?

MUSTARD: No, I just go out the front door.

SADIE: Okay. I'm not going to watch then. I'm not very good with people
leaving out the front door.

MUSTARD: Goodbye.

*He offers his hand. She looks at it, then slowly kisses him on the
cheek. The gesture means a lot to both of them. We get the feeling
this relationship was just getting started.*

SADIE: Begone.

SADIE goes to her room. THAI comes back in from the kitchen with a sandwich. MUSTARD is caught red-handed with his tiny suitcase. She looks at him. Makes a choice.

MUSTARD: Hey. This is awkward. I guess you caught me trying to leave without saying goodbye. I thought it'd be easier but now it just seems silly . . .

She walks past him.

Are you mad . . . ? Thai?

She goes upstairs. He follows her.

Thai?

Beat.

Thai?

THAI shuts the door as he's just about to come in, as if she didn't see him behind her. She sits in her chair, studiously not seeing him.

I'm right . . . here. I'm here.

THAI turns her face away, pretends not to see MUSTARD. It is very, very difficult for her.

I'm here. I'm HERE.

Beat.

Can you not see me? Can you *really* not see me, or are you just pretending? Because I'm going anyway. I'm going, you don't have to pretend. I get it, you need to be different.

THAI turns her face away from him again.

And . . . I want to protect you so you don't turn into . . . I'm already *going*. Please don't pretend. Please?

Beat.

You said you'd see me. You said you'd *always* see me.

MUSTARD starts to go. THAI can't bear it and picks up his hat from the ground where he left it a few scenes ago. She is devastated, but still trying to maintain the illusion that she can't see or hear him.

THAI: You forgot your hat.

She holds it out in his general direction. He goes to grab it but she doesn't let go, still not looking at him. They hold it together for a moment.

Promise you'll come back.

Beat.

MUSTARD: I *promise.*

THAI climbs into bed.

I love you, you dumb ugly poopy idiot. And I love this fucking hat.

BUG and LESLIE appear. BUG takes MUSTARD's suitcase. MUSTARD is devastated, but BUG and LESLIE are surprisingly amiable. MUSTARD clutches his flashlight.

BUG: You're doing a good thing, mister.

MUSTARD: It doesn't feel good.

LESLIE: The best things don't.

MUSTARD: I'm going to come back, you know. Not to visit, for good. I'm going to fight.

LESLIE: Fighting's not the same as winning.

BUG: But it's something to do, *(very pleased with himself)* nonetheless.

LESLIE: Nonetheless—very good, Bug.

BUG: Thank you, Leslie. Shall we?

LESLIE: Comeback. One word or two?

BUG: Comeback. / Comeback.

MUSTARD: Comeback. / Comeback.

LESLIE: Comeback. One, I think, Bug.

BUG: Sounds about right.

> Beat. MUSTARD *turns on his flashlight.*

MUSTARD: I think it can go either way.

> *Lights fade.*

> *The light of the flashlight sweeps over the dark of the theatre.*

> *We hear the jingle of* MUSTARD's *hat.*

> *End of play.*

ACKNOWLEDGEMENTS

Thank you to Richard Rose and everyone at Tarragon Theatre, especially the members of the 2014 Playwrights Unit, Andrea Romaldi and Andrea Donaldson. Thank you to Ashlie Corcoran for bringing this show to life in 2016 in the most generous, fun way possible, and for being such an inspiring, hard-working imagination machine. Thank you to Tom McGee for being a creative rock, and to all the brilliant actors and friends who read and shaped this play, including Daniel Pagett, Tim Walker, Claire Armstrong, Andy Trithardt, Tennille Read, Benjamin Blais, Jakob Ehman, Megan Miles, Caroline Toal, Scott Garland, Colin Munch, Caitlin Driscoll, the cast and creative team of the Arts Club production. Thank you to the incredible cast and creative / technical teams behind the original production for making me giggle every day in rehearsal and making the impossible possible. Thank you to Laura Anne Harris for keeping it all straight, Joel Bernbaum for his encouragement (and lending us the baby) and David Jansen for his insight. Thank you to my little sister, Alex, for putting up with me through our childhood, and, most of all, thank you to my parents, Ann and Jerry.

Kat Sandler is a writer, director and Artistic Director of Theatre Brouhaha. She has written fifteen original plays since 2011, and directed fourteen of them. She was a member of the 2014 Tarragon Playwrights Unit, where she developed *Mustard*, which won the 2016 Dora Mavor Moore Award for Outstanding New Play (General Division), and her play *Bang Bang* was nominated for the same award in 2018. She was the 2015 recipient of *NOW Magazine*'s Audience Choice Award for Best Director and Best Playwright. Kat is a graduate of the Queen's University drama program. She lives in Toronto, Ontario, and writes in coffee shops and bars.

First edition: November 2018
Printed and bound in Canada by Rapido Books, Montreal

Cover design by Leah Renihan
Author photo © Joseph Michael Photography

**PLAYWRIGHTS
CANADA PRESS**

202-269 Richmond St. W.
Toronto, ON
M5V 1X1

416.703.0013
info@playwrightscanada.com
www.playwrightscanada.com
@playcanpress